Teens and Drunk Driving

Look for these and other books in the Lucent
Teen Issues and Overview series:

Teen Alcoholism
Teen Depression
Teen Dropouts
Teen Drug Abuse
Teen Eating Disorders
Teen Parenting
Teen Pregnancy
Teen Prostitution
Teens and Divorce
Teens and Drunk Driving
Teen Sexuality
Teen Smoking
Teen Suicide
Teen Violence

Teens and Drunk Driving

by Nathan Aaseng

TEEN ISSUES

LUCENT Overview Series

Library of Congress Cataloging-in-Publication Data

Aaseng, Nathan.
    Teens and drunk driving / by Nathan Aaseng.
        p.   cm. — (Lucent overview series. Teen issues)
    Includes bibliographical references and index.
    Summary: Examines teens and drunk driving, discussing how
drinking affects driving ability, who drinks and drives and why, the
law and drunk driving, and preventing drunk driving tragedies.
    ISBN 1-56006-518-4 (lib. bdg. : alk. paper)
    1. Drinking and traffic accidents—United States—Juvenile
literature.   2. Drunk driving—United States—Juvenile literature
3. Teenagers—Alcohol use—United States—Juvenile literature
[1. Drinking and traffic accidents. 2. Drunk driving.]   I. Title.
II. Series.
HE5620.D72A27   2000
363.12'514'08350973—dc21   99-16888
                                          CIP

Contents

Introduction

No ONE AT Barron High School seemed to know exactly when the four ducked out of class on the morning of February 27, 1996. High school juniors Wonzel Crowe, Jeremy Whitman, and Jasper Stamper, and senior Saulo Rodriguez were not problem students. In fact, they were some of the highest young achievers in this rural community of about three thousand people in northwestern Wisconsin. Rodriguez reigned as the conference wrestling champion at 119 pounds and had recently placed fifth in the state meet. Stamper looked forward to improving on his school record 6-foot, 5-inch high jump during the spring track season. Crowe had earned a reputation for working hard and was being primed to take over the beef cattle farm that had been in the family for five generations.

But for some reason, the four were in a reckless party mood on that frosty winter morning. On their way to school, Crowe and Stamper had stopped by the home of 17-year-old Joshua McEwen. There they purchased a bottle of whiskey and a bottle of brandy for $20. Sometime after reporting for school, Crowe, Stamper, Whitman, and Rodriguez took off in Crowe's 1989 Ford Ranger.

An icy road

At about 10:45 that morning, John Elam drove his community sanitation truck out on the highway on his daily rounds. About a mile northeast of Barron, he came upon Crowe's vehicle, which was approaching at a high rate of speed from the east. The Ford Ranger swerved from its lane and then spun out of control. It slid several hundred yards on the ice-covered road before slamming broadside into the garbage truck. The impact was so devastating that it knocked the heavy truck on its side. Elam suffered only minor injuries. But amid the shattered glass and twisted wreckage of the pickup, all four high school boys lay dead of massive injuries.

Finding glass from a liquor bottle in Stamper's lap, investigators immediately suspected that drinking was the cause of the accident. State laboratory blood tests confirmed that all four had been drinking. Crowe, who was driving, had a blood alcohol content of nearly twice the level at which a driver is legally considered intoxicated.

Why?

News of the tragedy stunned the Barron community. More than a thousand people crammed the high school gym to pay their last respects to the victims. When the shock began to wear off, they began to ask how such a thing could have happened to these fine young men. How could this senseless slaughter have been avoided? Who was to blame?

Legal authorities zeroed in on Joshua McEwen, who had supplied the four with liquor. McEwen eventually pleaded

The Barron tragedy was not an isolated case. Here a Vermont state trooper examines a car in which four teens from Newport died while drinking and driving.

guilty to misdemeanor charges of contributing to the delinquency of a minor. The court sentenced him to six months in jail, three years' probation, and $2,000 in restitution. "I didn't mean to bring anyone harm by what I did,"[1] he told the court.

The remorse was all too familiar to the judge, who noted, "Most people end up here because they didn't think about the consequences of their actions."[2] The same words applied to the four young men, who were ultimately responsible for their own behavior. Crowe's sister, Aliesha Harelstad, tried to get this message across to local high school students. "My brother thought he was invincible. But the fact is that there are a lot of things that can happen, especially if you don't make responsible choices."[3]

Unbearable consequences

A lot of things can happen to someone who chooses to drink and drive, and almost all of them are bad: death, serious injury, jail, heavy fines, suspension of driving privileges, the weight of a guilty conscience, or nightmares that will not go away. Worst of all, by ignoring the risks of drinking and driving, Crowe, Whitman, Stamper, and Rodriguez brought unspeakable anguish to those who loved them. Rodriguez's father, Nicolas, pleaded with young people to wake up to the dangers of drinking and driving. "Spare your friends, teachers, and family the pain of a fatal mistake," he said. "More specifically, your parents, who might, like myself . . . have to carry the heavy burden of not being able to say to my son, 'I love you, Saulo.'"[4]

Unfortunately, despite many such warnings and strict laws that prohibit the consumption of liquor by teenagers, teens continue to drink and drive. Every year thousands of parents and siblings have to go through the anguish that gripped Nicolas Rodriguez and Aliesha Harelstad. Thousands more will have their lives shattered when a loved one is an innocent victim of someone else who drinks and drives.

1

Unguided Missiles on the Road

A PERSON WHO is shown a brand new gun will immediately recognize it as a weapon—a dangerous piece of equipment with the power to maim or kill. If that same person is shown a shiny new automobile, the reaction will be vastly different. He or she may feel admiration, excitement, desire, or envy. But it is a rare person who will immediately recognize the car as a destructive weapon. Yet, as Sergeant David Williams of the Monroe, North Carolina, police force puts it, "A person can die whether he ate a bullet from a nine-millimeter or from a 3,000-pound vehicle."[5] In fact, far more teenagers are killed by cars than by bullets.

In the United States, at any given moment there are millions of three-thousand-pound vehicles weaving through crowded city streets at thirty-five miles per hour or rocketing through the countryside at twice that speed. Society entrusts the lives and property of its citizens to the drivers of these vehicles. A driver is willing to merge into a stream of traffic only because he or she assumes that the other drivers are alert and in command of their vehicles.

When drivers are not in total control of their senses, their automobiles turn into occupied, unguided missiles that could plow into a tree, a building, an approaching car, or an innocent bystander at any time. These missiles are far more dangerous than guns, for, as Ricardo Martinez, head of the National Highway Traffic Safety Administration

(NHTSA), points out, they can "kill a family of four in one-tenth of a second, faster than a machine gun."[6]

It is no secret that drinking alcohol robs people of control of their senses. Yet, according to Dr. Dwight Heath, an anthropologist at Brown University, "There was a time when drunk driving was treated pretty much as a joke, like some kid caught with his hand in the cookie jar."[7]

An ancient and widespread custom

Part of the reason why people shrugged off drinking and driving for many years was because the use of alcoholic beverages is a firmly established tradition that dates back to prehistoric times. Descriptions of alcoholic beverages have been found in documents in India dating back four thousand years ago. In the ancient societies of both the Greeks and the Romans, alcohol became such an accepted part of social activity that their myths and legends include stories about gods of wine. Virtually all societies in the world have made use of some form of alcoholic beverage, although in the case of many Native American and Arab peoples, these products were unknown until brought in by other cultures.

In every society, alcohol has brought with it serious problems—ranging from addiction to violent, destructive, and irresponsible behavior, to disease and early death. Occasionally, groups have arisen attempting to eliminate or discourage the use of alcoholic beverages. Nevertheless, alcohol has held firm in its popularity throughout recorded history. In past centuries, alcoholic beverages were so commonly used in certain areas, especially in urban areas where the quality of the water was questionable, that they came to be identified with the particular culture. For Germans, the liquid refreshment of choice was beer; for the French, meals were not complete unless served with wine. Even in the unspoiled wilderness of North America, settlers generally considered alcoholic drinks to be safer and healthier than water.

In most people's minds, the potential dangers of alcohol did not appear to be serious enough to require any government regulation, not even for the young. As late as 1886, children in England could buy any alcoholic beverage on the market, although it was assumed they were buying them for their parents.

Drinking and motorized transportation

Until the invention of motorized transportation, drinking travelers posed no particular danger to the public. When the only way for the average person to travel was by walking, rowing a boat, or riding a horse, an intoxicated person's lack of judgment and coordination could get him or her in trouble but was not likely to hurt someone else. Even a runaway, riderless horse usually had the sense to avoid collisions. Except in cases of freak accidents, the

Drunk driving was once treated as a joke, as this staged photograph from the 1940s demonstrates.

only people vulnerable to harm from drunk drivers were those who chose to ride in ships or carriages driven by hired hands who had been drinking.

As motorized transportation became popular, however, people began to realize the potential for destruction that lay at the hands of a drunken operator. As early as 1843, the New York Central Railroad formally banned the drinking of alcoholic beverages by any employee on duty.

The invention of the automobile in the late nineteenth century marked the first time that great numbers of individuals took command of powerful, heavy, fast-moving vehicles. Along with ready access to this speed and power came the danger of terrible collisions. In the final years of the nineteenth century, the United States recorded its first automobile fatality. As the trickle of automobiles on the roads turned into a flood of traffic, death tolls soared into the thousands.

As more and more people began to rely on their own automobiles for transportation, the drinking of alcoholic beverages posed a danger that society had never before experienced. It produced a large number of unsafe operators of dangerous vehicles. Henry Ford, who was one of the individuals most responsible for bringing the automobile into the hands of the average American, found the possibilities so frightening that he predicted alcohol would disappear from society. In his view, "booze had to go when modern industry and the motor car came in."[8]

Although few others were so extreme in their views, most people recognized that drunken automobile operators presented a serious danger to the public. The state of New York added the offense of drunk driving to its traffic regulations in 1910. California was among many states that enacted laws prior to World War I that provided that those who drove drunk could be put in jail or their driving privileges suspended.

The problem grows

Enforcement of drunk driving laws in the first half of the twentieth century, however, was spotty. There were no tests available to determine how much alcohol was in a person's system. Therefore, arrest and conviction for a drunk driving offense depended on a police officer's guess of how intoxicated the driver was. Unless a person displayed the most obvious signs of drunkenness, such as slurred speech, incoherent mumbling, and poor balance, drunk driving was difficult to prove. Furthermore, drinking and driving was commonly viewed as one of those wild and crazy things that ordinary, fun-loving people occasionally do from time to time. The lack of concern over teens' drinking and driving is evidenced by the almost complete absence of reporting on the subject.

In the 1950s, scientists began to develop accurate chemical tests that could determine the amount of alcohol in the bloodstream. This made arrests and convictions for driving while intoxicated easier to obtain. But it did not seem to stem the tide of drunk driving. Less than half a century after it was first declared illegal, driving while intoxicated had become the nation's most commonly prosecuted offense in court.

During the 1960s, the U.S. Department of Transportation came out with a stunning report, called "Alcohol and Highway Safety," that opened the nation's eyes to the seriousness of the drunk driving problem. This report estimated that twenty-five thousand people were being killed on U.S. streets and highways each year by drunk drivers. Although many experts questioned the accuracy of this figure, the mind-boggling number of reported deaths led to the launching of federal programs aimed at reducing drinking and driving.

Lowering the drinking age

However, even though public awareness of drunk driving increased in the 1970s, the problem grew even worse because of changes in state drinking laws that arose in response to the Vietnam War. The war was unpopular, particularly with young people. They protested against the fact that the government could send teenagers to fight and die in the war but yet those teens had no voice in choosing the

A victim of a drunk driver is pulled from the wreckage of his car in the 1950s. As people began to rely more on their own cars, the idea of drinking and driving became more frightening.

people who made such decisions. If they were old enough to take on the burden of fighting and dying in the nation's wars, teens argued, they should be treated as adults and not children. They particularly sought the right to vote. During the 1970s, society agreed with them. All states lowered their voting age requirement to eighteen.

Once the voting right was extended to the young, people questioned why any other adult privileges should be denied to eighteen-year-olds. It appeared simpler and more reasonable to establish eighteen as the legal starting point of adulthood. Taking this point of view, many states in the 1970s also lowered their legal drinking age to eighteen.

Unfortunately, the effects of this last change led to a slaughter of young people on the highways. Teenagers began drinking and driving in record numbers. Injuries and deaths among young drivers soared. In 1964, government analysts had estimated 7,797 deaths of teenagers as a result of drunk driving. By 1975, the annual toll had jumped to nearly 9,000.

Attacking the problem

Shocked by the mounting death toll, some individuals began to take action. In 1979, after a local teenager died from injuries caused by a drunk driver, Doris Aiken of Schenectady, New York, organized a group called Remove Intoxicated Drivers (RID). A year later, thirteen-year-old Cari Lightner of Fair Oaks, California, was walking with a friend when she was killed by a drunk driver. Candy Lightner's grief turned to rage when she learned that the man who killed her daughter had been arrested only two days earlier and charged with his third drunk driving offense. Determined to keep such irresponsible drivers off the road, she formed Mothers Against Drunk Driving (MADD). In March 1983, NBC carried her story to the nation by broadcasting a movie about her tragic experience. Both RID and MADD worked hard to call attention to the misery caused by drunk drivers and fought for laws protecting the public from them.

At the same time, lawmakers recognized the destruction that resulted from the lowered drinking age. From 1976 to 1980, eleven states raised their drinking age back to nineteen, twenty, or twenty-one. This left the nation with a jumble of drinking laws that varied from state to state. The situation created a particularly dangerous drunk driving hazard around state borders. Teens from a state with a high drinking age flocked across the border to a state where they could legally drink. They almost always had to drive home after a night of partying and often were in no condition to be on the highways. More tragedy resulted.

In 1984, the federal government took dramatic action to solve the problem. Congress passed legislation requiring states to raise their legal drinking age to twenty-one in order to be eligible for federal highway construction funds. Many people grumbled that the federal government had no right to dictate what states had to do. But since no state could afford to pass up millions of dollars in federal construction money, all thirty-seven states with drinking ages below twenty-one raised their legal drinking standards to twenty-one by the end of the 1980s.

Teen drunk driving today

The efforts of groups such as MADD and RID, government agencies, and other organizations have paid off in greater awareness today of the hazards of drunk driving. This, combined with the laws raising the minimum legal drinking age to twenty-one, has led to a decline in the numbers of people who drink and drive. Arrests for driving under the influence had been climbing in the early 1980s, to a peak of 1.9 million in 1983. Since then, they have fallen steadily, to fewer than 1.5 million in 1996. The decline is all

Buttons issued by MADD strongly advise drivers to avoid mixing alcohol and automobiles.

the more remarkable because the number of drivers on the roads and the amount of miles they drive have increased.

Statistics show that teens have been most responsible for the drop in drunk driving arrests. In the '90s, teenagers dramatically turned their backs on drinking as a regular activity. In 1990 the National Household Survey on Drug Abuse reported that 32.5 percent of teens ages twelve to seventeen reported using alcohol at least once in the past month. When the survey was repeated in 1996, the number dropped to 18.8 percent. As a result of less drinking, fewer teens have been caught driving while under the influence. According to statistics from the NHTSA, in 1980, drivers between the ages of sixteen and twenty made up about 10 percent of the U.S. licensed driving population, yet they accounted for 15 percent of arrests for driving under the influence (DUI). In other words, teens were drinking and driving far more often than the average driver. In 1996, teen drivers made up 7 percent of the nation's licensed drivers and were responsible for only 8 percent of the DUI arrests. This showed that teens were only slightly more likely than other age groups to engage in drinking and driving.

A modern success story

Efforts by individuals and government agencies to reduce drinking and driving have saved thousands of lives and billions of dollars in property damages over the past decade. In 1986, alcohol was cited as a factor in roughly twenty-four thousand traffic fatalities, more than half of all motor vehicle deaths. Ten years later, use of alcohol was involved in nearly 7,000 fewer deaths, less than 41 percent of the 1996 traffic death toll.

The trend of reduced teen drinking and driving has been especially noticeable in the 1990s. Before states raised the legal drinking age in the '80s, drinking and driving was the number one cause of death among teens. Since the mid-1980s, motor vehicle accidents in which alcohol is *not* involved have taken over as the number one killer of teens. Alcohol-related traffic deaths for young people were cut in half from 22 deaths per 100,000 in the early 1980s to 11 per 100,000 in the mid-1990s. Reduction in the accidents involving drivers who were seriously drunk accounted for all of the decline.

In raw numbers, 8,508 young people lost their lives in traffic accidents in 1982. Twelve years later, the number of teens killed in motor vehicle accidents during the year declined to 6,226 teenagers, a savings of well over 2,000 lives. As the NHTSA notes, "Few social programs aimed at reducing mortality can measure success with the magnitude of these numbers."[9]

Still a national tragedy

As encouraging as the downward trend of teen drunk driving may be, the fight is far from over. Despite a constant barrage of publicity against drinking and driving, and the fact that drinking alcoholic beverages is illegal for all teens, young people continue to drink and drive more than most other age groups of drivers. This is especially true of older teens. In a recent survey, more than half the first-year students at Boston area colleges admitted that, during the past year, they had driven after drinking alcohol.

Although fewer teenagers drink and drive than did a decade ago, those who do continue to cause more tragedy and destruction than drunk drivers in other age groups. The number of teens killed in alcohol-related motor vehicle accidents continues to hover about 10 percent above the national average for alcohol-related deaths. According to the NHTSA, alcohol continues to be a factor in over 35 percent of all teen motor vehicle fatalities.

"We think of all the things Dana won't see"

Statistically speaking, a drop from eight thousand to six thousand may be cause for celebration. But those six thousand deaths, every one of them needless and avoidable, still leave a broad trail of grief in their wakes. Each spins a tale of misery and human suffering like that experienced by the family of Dana Ogletree of Brooks, Georgia. On the morning of December 20, 1995, Shandra

Young People, Drinking, and Driving

▶ Eight young people a day die in alcohol-related crashes. (CSAP, 1996)

▶ Younger people (ages 16–20) are most likely of any age group to use various strategies, when hosting a social occasion where alcohol is served, to try to prevent their guests from drinking and driving. (NHTSA, 1996)

▶ 7,738 intoxicated drivers (.10 BAC or greater) between the ages of 16 and 20 were fatally injured in 1995. (NHTSA, 1996)

▶ Between 1985 and 1995, the proportion of drivers 16 to 20 years of age who were involved in fatal crashes, and were intoxicated, dropped 47 percent—23.9 percent in 1985 to 12.7 percent in 1994—the largest decrease of any age group during this time period. (NHTSA, 1996)

Source: MADD.

Ogletree said goodbye to her husband as he headed off to work, just as she had most mornings of their nineteen-year marriage. She had no idea that she would never see him alive again.

Ogletree was driven to work that day by his coworker David Harris. On the way to their job, Harris took a detour to deliver his fiancée's three young children to the home of their father. Before they reached their first stop, a seventeen-year-old driver who was drunk on beer rammed their car broadside at a high speed. Ogletree was rushed to the hospital where emergency surgery was performed, but it was not enough to save him; he died the following morning. Harris and the three children were also killed.

In an instant, a foolish decision by a teenager shattered the lives of dozens of people. Although sentenced to ten years in prison, the driver got off much easier than any of his victims. Dana Ogletree's five children were left without a father and will be haunted by that senseless loss for the rest of their lives. Even the happiest occasions of their lives will be tinged in sorrow because, as Shandra said, "We think of all the things Dana won't see." [10]

Keeping the pressure on

The encouraging reduction in drunk driver fatalities over the past decade provides no comfort to people such as the Ogletrees. Nor is there any guarantee that the progress of the last decade will continue. Americans tend to focus on issues for a short amount of time before the subject becomes stale and the media look for fresher, more sensational stories. Furthermore, despite the progress made, people still tend to underestimate the seriousness of drunk driving. Most people are far more worried about being killed in their homes by an intruder than they are about being run down by a drunk driver, despite statistics that show the danger from drunk drivers is far greater. The demand for protection from violent crime and household intruders puts pressure on police forces to pour more of their limited funds into pre-

Donna Shalala urges vigilance against drunk driving.

venting burglaries. According to law-enforcement experts, this means that there is less money to spend on traffic law enforcement.

Donna Shalala, secretary for Health and Human Services, argues that the nation cannot afford to become complacent about the tragic effects of drinking and driving: "This is no time to underfund these programs. This is the time to step forward and continue the momentum that we've created."[11]

2

How Drinking Affects Driving Ability

THE ALCOHOL PRESENT in beer, wine, whiskey, and other liquors is known as ethyl alcohol, or ethanol. Ethanol is a thin, colorless liquid with a strong aroma that has a dramatic effect on the nervous system. It is formed naturally when tiny living organisms known as yeast react with sugars at warm temperatures.

Entering the bloodstream

When a person drinks alcoholic beverages, the ethanol quickly enters the bloodstream without being chemically changed in any way. About 20 percent of it passes directly into the bloodstream from the stomach; the rest is absorbed through the small intestines. The speed with which it is absorbed depends on a number of factors. For example, the absorption rate is slower when food is present in the stomach. Also, alcohol mixed with other liquids such as water or soda is absorbed more slowly than highly concentrated alcohol.

Once ethanol enters the bloodstream, there is no way to remove it quickly. Popular techniques for "sobering up" a person, such as strong coffee or a cold shower, have absolutely no effect. Only the steady action of the liver, which can convert ethanol into carbohydrates, will cleanse the blood. Generally, an average-sized person is able to remove alcohol from the bloodstream at the rate of about an ounce per hour.

Blood Alcohol Concentration Within One Hour

number of drinks

weight in pounds	1	2	3	4	5
100	.04	.09	.15	.20	.25
120	.03	.08	.12	.16	.21
140	.02	.06	.10	.14	.18
160	.02	.05	.09	.12	.15
180	.02	.05	.08	.10	.13
200	.01	.04	.07	.09	.12

0 to .04
Not legally under the influence. Impairment possible.

.05 to .09
State laws regarding BAC legal limits vary. Mental and physical impairment noticeable.

.10 and above
Presumed intoxicated in all 50 states.

Figures are rounded to nearest .01. BACs shown are approximate, since they can be affected by factors other than weight.

Source: National Clearinghouse for Alcohol and Drug Information.

Measuring drunkenness

The presence of a very small amount of ethanol in the bloodstream has a dramatic impact on the nervous system. One of the reasons for this, according to Vivian Begali in *Head Injury in Children and Adolescents*, is that the brain is "completely dependent upon blood for its oxygen" and "at any given time, the brain contains approximately 20 per cent of the body's total blood supply."[12] A teaspoonful of alcohol in the entire blood supply can completely change a person's personality and ability to function. When alcohol in the bloodstream reaches a level of only one-half of 1 percent, the result is almost always fatal. Therefore, when measuring the amount of alcohol in a person's system, analysts are working with extremely small numbers.

The standard measurement of the presence of alcohol in a person's system is the blood alcohol content (BAC). A BAC of .10 means that alcohol makes up one-tenth of 1 percent of the total volume of the blood.

The terms *drunk* and *intoxicated* are not scientific, and there is no precise definition that fits all cases. Alcohol affects different people in different ways. Studies have shown that even police officers, who have considerable training and experience in dealing with heavy drinkers, cannot always tell when a person is under the influence of alcohol.

Because drunkenness is difficult to determine just by a person's appearance and behavior, authorities have come to rely heavily on the BAC as the standard for determining whether or not a person is intoxicated. Most states consider a BAC of .10 as the dividing line between being sober and being drunk. Canada and several states enforce .08 as the legal limit.

What does it take for a person to get drunk?

For an average person, one ounce of alcohol will produce a BAC of .02. Two cans of beer, a seven-ounce glass of wine, and a two-ounce shot of whiskey all contain about an ounce of alcohol. That means that a person would require ten beers, five glasses of wine, or five drinks of liquor to reach .10, the legal level of intoxication in most states.

While that sounds like a large amount of alcohol in a short amount of time, there are several factors involved that create problems for many drinkers. First, the slow rate at which the body removes alcohol from the bloodstream puts those who drink during the course of a long evening at risk. A person who consumes four drinks in the first hour to stay under the legal limit and then cuts back to two drinks an hour for the next three hours may feel he or she is being responsible. But in reality, the drinker has added six ounces of alcohol to the four already in his or her system, while the body has been able to remove only three. That makes a total of seven ounces, which would produce a BAC of roughly .14, well over the legal limit.

Furthermore, a person's physical makeup greatly affects BAC. A smaller person circulates less blood than a larger person does, so an ounce of alcohol will make up a greater proportion of his or her total blood. This means that a small person may reach a BAC of .10 on three or four drinks rather than five. Also, those with a higher percentage of body fat will reach a high BAC more quickly than those whose bodies are more lean and muscular.

Since the presence of food in the stomach reduces the rate at which the body absorbs alcohol, those who eat while drinking will not reach high BAC levels as quickly as those who drink on an empty stomach. Body chemistry and state of mind can also affect the rate at which a person's BAC climbs.

Because the body absorbs strong concentrations of alcohol more quickly than diluted alcohol, a person who drinks straight whiskey or vodka will reach a high BAC more

Body chemistry and state of mind are among the factors that influence the effects of even one glass of liquor.

Source: National Clearinghouse for Alcohol and Drug Information.

The Amount of Alcohol in One Drink

 12 ounces of beer (5% alcohol)

 5 ounces of wine (12% alcohol)

 1.5 ounces of liquor (40% alcohol)

Each of the three types of alcohol listed above has about the same amount of ethyl alcohol—**.6 ounces**.

quickly than one who drinks the same amount of alcohol from beer, which is mostly water, or mixed drinks. Combined with the fact that beer has an alcohol content only about one-tenth that of strong liquor, this has led many people to consider beer a fairly "safe" alcoholic beverage. However, people tend to drink beer in far greater amounts than they do other alcoholic beverages. The fact is that a person who drinks a great deal of beer can get just as drunk as a person who drinks strong liquor.

How alcohol affects the brain

Even though many people think of alcohol as a stimulant because it helps them reach a state of excitement or contentment known as a "high," it is actually the opposite. Alcohol is a depressant. It slows down or reduces the efficiency of many of the activities of the nervous system.

Alcohol has a strong effect on the part of the brain that governs wakefulness. Many people find that even a single glass of wine makes them drowsy. People with a very high BAC run a good risk of passing out altogether.

Alertness is a related function of the brain that describes a general state of readiness to receive and process information. By slowing down the response rate of the nervous system, alcohol leaves people less aware of their surroundings, less able to focus attention beyond a brief period of time, and less efficient in gathering information from the senses.

Alcohol and judgment

One of the most important functions of the human brain is judgment. The brain collects data from all the senses, compares them with past experiences, and comes up with an appropriate reaction to the countless situations that come up during a day. Many of these situations are trivial, and the brain can handle them without the person's even being conscious of making a decision. For example, when someone climbs a flight of stairs, the brain measures the height of the steps and signals the muscles to raise the legs to the needed level to reach the next step. The required reaction is so routine that the climber does not even think about raising the legs. Situations that are less routine involve more conscious thought. A person driving in an unfamiliar city, for example, must make conscious decisions of where to turn.

Every decision the brain makes, whether conscious or unconscious, occurs because of electrical and chemical impulses sent through the nerve network. Alcohol slows down and may even block these impulses. This blockage may also reduce or blot out a person's memory, robbing him or her of the storehouse of experience upon which decisions are based. By causing problems with the nervous system, alcohol makes it difficult for people to process the information they receive from their senses and make appropriate responses. Even when they respond instinctively to situations, their reaction time is considerably slower than it would have been without the presence of alcohol.

Alcohol and restraint

A surprisingly large amount of brain activity is concerned not with taking action but with restraining natural impulses. For example, when a person sees an expensive watch in a store, a natural response may be a strong desire to have that watch. If the brain were concerned only with satisfying that desire, the person would impulsively steal the watch. However, most people understand that they cannot simply act to satisfy whatever desire arises. Through a long process of socialization, the brain has learned which behaviors are appropriate and which are not. Recognizing that taking the watch will bring undesirable consequences, the brain acts to inhibit that natural impulse.

While the brain's ability to restrain a person's natural impulses helps him or her to cope with the demands of society, this restraint can be so overpowering that people often feel stifled by it. Many people feel so inhibited, particularly in social situations, that they are afraid to take any chances at all. They end up unable to make conversation, to have fun, and to "be themselves."

One of the attractions of alcohol is that it depresses the inhibiting powers of the brain. With the restraints eased, people often feel more relaxed and carefree. This accounts for the "high" that alcohol produces. However, when those restraints are dulled, a person is also more likely to take dangerous chances and to be rude, offensive, and even violent to others.

The consumption of alcohol affects a person's judgment, memory, reaction time, and restraint.

Similarly, alcohol reduces the brain's ability to keep emotions under control. An intoxicated person is more likely to experience uncontrollable anger, sadness, or joy.

Alcohol and eyesight

Alcohol does not have any apparent effect on the sharpness of a person's vision. However, it does tend to narrow the field of vision. A person under the influence of alcohol loses some peripheral vision—the ability to see what is happening off to the side.

Alcohol also affects the eyes' ability to adjust to light. The pupils regulate the amount of light entering the eyes by enlarging when it is dark and shrinking under bright light. Alcohol interferes with the ability of the pupils to regulate incoming light. A brief exposure to bright light can cause an intoxicated person to be virtually blind for several seconds.

Alcohol and coordination

Since the nervous system controls the actions of the muscles, any reduction in the efficiency of the brain leads to reduced coordination. Those under the influence of alcohol may have problems walking in a straight line, avoiding objects, maintaining balance, and manipulating objects with their fingers. Performing relatively simple tasks such as jumping rope, hammering a nail, or even picking up a glass from a table may be difficult.

Effects of drinking on driving

Many of alcohol's effects on the nervous system have a direct impact on driving ability. Vehicles today often travel at high speeds and in heavy traffic. Drivers must be alert to frequently posted signs regulating traffic and warning them of dangers ahead. At busy intersections, traffic may come at the driver from at least four directions. Vehicles may shift lanes, enter from side streets or driveways, or suddenly stop with little or no warning. Bicycles and pedestrians and hazardous road conditions may further complicate the situation. A driver must be alert at

Alcohol reduces a person's ability to drive safely at high speeds and in heavy traffic.

all times to this constantly changing scene because a single unexpected event can cause a serious accident.

Alcohol puts drivers at risk by making them sleepy and dulling their overall senses. Intoxicated drivers have trouble focusing on the task of driving and often fail to pay attention to signs and to the movements of others. Tests have proven that the more a person drinks, the slower the reactions. This can prove deadly, for example, in a case in which a child darts out into a street. A sober person will hit the brake far more quickly than someone who has been drinking.

A moment's lapse in attention

The result of even a moment's lapse at the wheel can destroy lives, as seventeen-year-old Brandon Blenden discovered. On the evening of Super Bowl Sunday in January 1995, Blenden was driving along the streets of Gulfport, Mississippi, in his pickup. Not only had he been drinking heavily, but he was still drinking from a beer bottle wedged between his legs as he approached an intersection.

In front of him, Ann Lee pulled to a stop to let the cross-traffic clear. She was making a quick run to the grocery store with her four-year-old daughter, Whitney, buckled into the backseat. His senses dulled by alcohol, Blenden never noticed the stopped car in front of him, nor did it occur to him to slow down approaching the intersection. His pickup slammed into the rear of Lee's car, crushing it like an accordion. The collision sent Whitney Lee into a coma. Two days later, the little girl died.

Judgment and driving

The constantly shifting environment of traffic requires dozens of quick, clearheaded decisions. Drivers must be able to decide such life-and-death actions as whether they have room to pass a car on a highway, whether they have time to make a left turn in front of an oncoming bus, how to pull out of a skid on a slippery stretch of road, how much to slow down on a curve, whether they need to speed up or slow down to merge onto a busy freeway, or how hard to apply the brake when the car in front suddenly slows.

By clouding the brain's judgment, alcohol places the driver, any passengers, and those around him or her in deadly danger of the driver's making the wrong decision in any of these situations, as well as many others.

Restraint and driving

Because of the potential for serious injury, anyone operating a motor vehicle needs to exercise caution at all times.

People who are high on alcohol, however, often feel freed from the usual inhibitions that protect them from acting on impulse. A sober person traveling behind a slow-moving car may feel irritated or frustrated at being delayed. However, he or she is not likely to act on that frustration by passing the car on a blind curve. An intoxicated person, on the other hand, may be unable to squelch the impulse.

The lack of self-restraint resulting from alcohol use can lead to dozens of deadly situations, such as driving forty miles over the speed limit, running a stop sign, weaving through traffic, and refusing to yield the right of way. This lack of restraint also means that drunk drivers are more likely to get angry at other drivers and purposely take actions that endanger them.

Vision and driving

Alcohol's effect on peripheral vision is especially dangerous to the operation of a motor vehicle. Many potential hazards of the road do not appear directly in front of the driver but, rather, come from the side. Drivers with good peripheral vision can recognize a car pulling out of a driveway and can take action before the car causes a problem. Intoxicated drivers are not likely to notice any potential problem until it actually appears in front of them. By then, in many cases, it may be too late.

Drinking alcohol adversely affects a driver's vision, especially at night.

An intoxicated driver's inability to adjust quickly to changes in light makes drunk driving at night especially dangerous. The glare of approaching headlights can cause a drunk driver to steer blindly for several seconds.

Coordination and driving

The act of driving requires precise coordination, particularly of the hands in steering and the foot in operating the accelerator and the brake. Even the basic task of keeping the vehicle on a straight course is often difficult for intoxicated drivers. They present a danger to others by frequently veering out of their lane and over the center dividing line and present a danger to themselves and their passengers by driving off the road. More difficult actions, such as swerving to avoid an object or a person, may be all but impossible to a person whose coordination is impaired by alcohol.

Levels of intoxication

Alcohol affects different people in different ways. In general, a person with a BAC of .05 does not show physical effects but will experience a reduction in the ability to think, react, make judgments, and restrain impulses. According to the American Medical Association's Committee of Medicolegal Problems, at .10 BAC, the legal level of intoxication for most states, half the population shows obvious signs of drunkenness. This includes some difficulty in hand-eye coordination, walking in a straight line, and maintaining balance, and slurred speech.

Individuals with a BAC of .20 generally display all of these problems in an obvious way. They have difficulty standing or walking at all. Emotional behavior is often severely affected. A person with this level of intoxication may be exceptionally loud or violent, or may cry or laugh uncontrollably. A .30 BAC affects the deeper thought processes. Those who drink to this level may not be able to understand simple questions and may be unaware of where they are or how they got there. BAC levels approaching .40 result in unconsciousness and possible death.

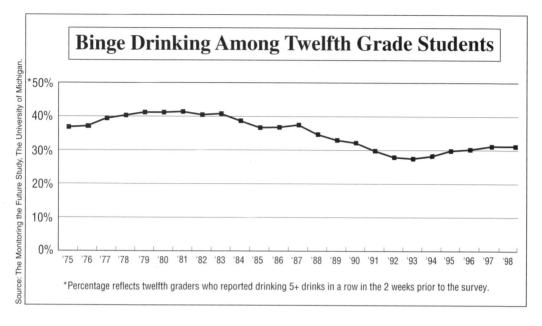

Binge Drinking Among Twelfth Grade Students

*50%

40%

30%

20%

10%

0%

'75 '76 '77 '78 '79 '80 '81 '82 '83 '84 '85 '86 '87 '88 '89 '90 '91 '92 '93 '94 '95 '96 '97 '98

*Percentage reflects twelfth graders who reported drinking 5+ drinks in a row in the 2 weeks prior to the survey.

"Safe" drinking and driving

Many people do not show any obvious physical effects of drinking at levels of .10 and below, and there are some individuals whose BAC can reach .20 before they show any of the more recognizable signs of intoxication. According to James Jacobs in *Drunk Driving: An American Dilemma*, "At a BAC of 0.10 some drivers can operate a vehicle with reasonable skill and judgment."[13] Because of this, people often make a distinction between "safe" social drinkers who can handle their liquor and reckless drunk drivers. They note that the average BAC of intoxicated drivers involved in fatal accidents is .16, a level that indicates irresponsible binge drinking. This fact, plus statistics showing that a person with a BAC of .15 runs one hundred times the risk of a nondrinker of being involved in a fatal crash, seems to indicate that drunk driving is a problem for alcohol abusers and not for social drinkers.

However, other experts such as H. Laurence Ross, author of *Confronting Drunk Driving*, argue that such an attitude is dangerous. Ross believes that *drunk driving* is a misleading term because it gives the impression that only those who are legally intoxicated pose a danger behind the wheel. He prefers the term *"alcohol impaired driving"*[14] to indicate that even moderate drinking reduces alertness, judgment, restraint, reaction time, and coordination enough to pose a risk to motorists.

Statistics show that a driver with a BAC of .05, which can result from only two or three typical drinks, is twice as likely as a nondrinker to be involved in a standard crash. For this reason, the National Institute on Alcohol Abuse and Alcoholism considers operating a vehicle at any BAC level above .05 as driving while impaired. At a BAC of .08, which most states consider low enough to allow operation of a motor vehicle, the risk is ten times that of the average driver. A driver with a BAC of .10, which is the border of the legally acceptable level in most states, is twenty times more likely than the average driver to suffer a fatal accident.

The U.S. Department of Transportation believes that even legal, socially acceptable levels of drinking cause a danger to the operation of motor vehicles. It has set .04 as the legal BAC limit for those involved in commercial transportation, such as truck driving.

Some studies have found even more persuasive evidence that social drinking and driving do not mix. A study conducted by the University of Kentucky found that as few as two drinks can seriously harm a person's driving performance. Researchers Herbert Moskowitz and Marceline Burns concluded that "Certain skills important for driving are impaired at .01 to .02 BAC or, in other words, at the lowest levels that can be measured reliably."[15] In other words, there is no distinct dividing line between a safe and an unsafe level of drinking and driving.

3

Who Drinks and Drives and Why

KEVIN TUNNELL HAD heard all the warnings about the dangers of drinking and driving. But none of that applied to him. After all, he could handle his liquor. Despite the fact that he was only seventeen and not legally old enough to drink, he had driven after drinking alcohol many times. In fact, he liked to brag to friends that he drove better when he was drunk.

On New Year's Eve, Tunnell went to a party where he celebrated the changing of the calendar by slurping down half a dozen glasses of champagne. Maybe it was seven or eight glasses. Shortly after 1 A.M., he left the party and drove off.

At 1:15, Susan Herzon waved goodbye to her boyfriend after leaving a party at his house and stepped into her Volkswagen. Unlike Tunnell, Herzon was not much of a drinker. Even though it was only a two-mile drive back to her home in Fairfax, Virginia, she had been careful to avoid alcohol that night. She was less than a mile from home when Tunnell roared down the highway toward her at fifty miles per hour in a thirty-mile-per-hour zone. Just before meeting Herzon's car, Tunnell swerved across the double-yellow line. He slammed into the Volkswagen so hard that he knocked it backwards twenty yards onto a lawn.

Herzon, vice president of her senior class and a top student, died from her injuries. Tunnell survived.

The typical drunk driver

In many ways, Tunnell fits the profile of the typical teenage drunk driver. According to Susan Herbel of the National Commission Against Drunk Driving, "Drunk driving is very much a male problem."[16] Estimates of the ratio of men to women who drink and drive reach as high as 9 to 1. Like Tunnell, drunk drivers tend to be white. They are most often frequent drivers who consider themselves good drivers, and frequent drinkers who take pride in their drinking. A Quincy, Massachusetts, study of more than a thousand court cases found that four out of five of those convicted of drunk driving were problem drinkers.

As in the Tunnell case, fatal accidents involving drunk drivers occur far more commonly at night than during the day, and on weekends and holidays than during weekdays. Drinking and driving takes place far more often in suburbs, such as Fairfax, and rural areas than it does in urban areas. New York City, for example, holds 40 percent of its state's population yet records only 3 percent of the state's drunk driving arrests. One survey found that 28 percent of those living in suburban areas and 29 percent of those living in upstate New York admitted to drinking and driving, compared with only 11 percent in New York City.

Also, despite the common image of drunk drivers as repeat offenders who are constantly drinking and driving, most drivers who are at fault in fatal vehicle crashes, like Tunnell, have no known prior arrests for drunk driving.

No profile fits all

Some aspects of this case, however, do not fit the most common drunk driving circumstances. Although alcohol-related crashes in which drunk drivers run into and kill innocent victims are the most tragic and receive the widest publicity, more than half of the fatalities in alcohol-related accidents involve single-car crashes. Most of those killed in alcohol-related accidents are the drunk drivers themselves.

In reality, drunk driving is a complex problem that defies simple profiles and simple answers. While males,

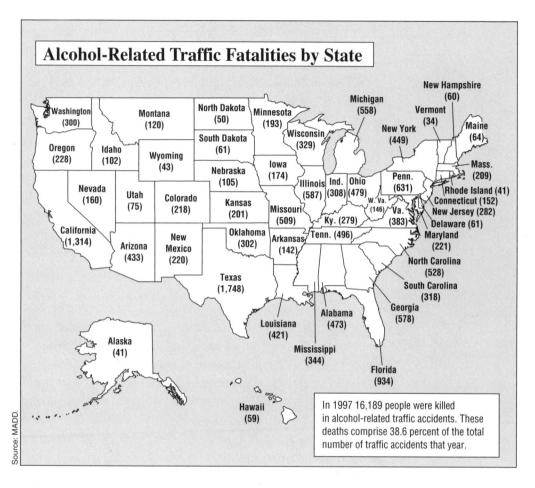

Alcohol-Related Traffic Fatalities by State

Washington (300)
Oregon (228)
Idaho (102)
Montana (120)
Wyoming (43)
North Dakota (50)
South Dakota (61)
Nebraska (105)
Minnesota (193)
Wisconsin (329)
Michigan (558)
New Hampshire (60)
Vermont (34)
New York (449)
Maine (64)
Nevada (160)
Utah (75)
Colorado (218)
Kansas (201)
Iowa (174)
Illinois (587)
Ind. (308)
Ohio (479)
Penn. (631)
Mass. (209)
Rhode Island (41)
Connecticut (152)
W. Va. (146)
Va. (383)
New Jersey (282)
Delaware (61)
California (1,314)
Arizona (433)
New Mexico (220)
Oklahoma (302)
Missouri (509)
Ky. (279)
Tenn. (496)
Arkansas (142)
Maryland (221)
North Carolina (528)
South Carolina (318)
Texas (1,748)
Louisiana (421)
Mississippi (344)
Alabama (473)
Georgia (578)
Florida (934)
Alaska (41)
Hawaii (59)

In 1997 16,189 people were killed in alcohol-related traffic accidents. These deaths comprise 38.6 percent of the total number of traffic accidents that year.

Source: MADD.

whites, problem drinkers, and suburban or rural drivers are more susceptible to drunk driving, alcohol-impaired drivers come from all walks of life. There is no single profile that fits all teenage drunk drivers and alcohol-related crashes.

Teen drinking

Since no state allows teens to legally drink, teen drinking and driving would not exist if people simply obeyed the law. Yet teenagers have been breaking the drinking laws for as long as they have been on the books.

There are encouraging signs that drinking among young people has been on the decline in recent years. Nevertheless, the Office of Juvenile Justice and Delinquency Prevention reported in 1996 that about 9.5 million U.S. teenagers admitted that they drank alcoholic beverages on occasion. Of this number, roughly 40 percent admitted to engaging in binge drinking, which can be defined as drinking in excess for the purpose of getting intoxicated. More than 20 percent described themselves as problem drinkers. According to statistics compiled in the same year by the Office of National Drug Control Policy, almost 45 percent of students in grades six through eight used alcohol in the past year. In other words, nearly half of the students had some experience with drinking well before they reached driving age. More than seven out of ten students in grades nine through twelve admitted to alcohol use in the past year.

Peer pressure to drink

Most teens cite peer pressure as the main reason why they start drinking in violation of the law. One of their friends invites or challenges them to drink. Unwilling to appear uncool or cowardly, teens often join in despite their initial reservations. While this sounds simple and straightforward, the reasons why teens create peer pressure in favor of drinking are more complex.

One of the most important factors is teens' desire to be accepted as grown-up and mature. Growing up is a long, gradual struggle for independence from parents. Throughout adolescence, young people become frustrated at being treated like small children with few rights and privileges of their own and in need of constant adult supervision. They want to be treated as responsible, capable adults, and they look forward to assuming the privileges that come with adulthood.

Society has established the drinking of alcoholic beverages as one of the most prominent privileges that comes with being an adult. That has not always been the case. In the earlier part of the twentieth century, a majority of Americans frowned on the use of alcoholic beverages. This disapproval was so strong that, in 1918, the nation passed a constitutional amendment banning the sale of any alcoholic beverage. But after these Prohibition laws were overturned in 1932, American consumption of alcohol rose steadily.

Presently, there is virtually no support for laws banning the sale of alcoholic beverages. More than two-thirds of all adults drink alcohol to some degree. Those who drink average three drinks per day, with most drinkers consuming less and heavy drinkers consuming far more. Many current customs and institutions not only allow drinking to take place but encourage it. Drinking has achieved such a popular status among adults that it has become a tempting target for teens claiming the adult status that they so desperately seek.

Why adults drink

The question of why teens drink cannot be answered without first considering why adults drink. For many

Prohibition proved unpopular even though a majority of Americans disapproved of alcohol.

adults, particularly those with European backgrounds, drinking is a tradition that dates back many generations. In countries such as France, Italy, and Germany, wine and beer are considered the standard drinks that go with meals.

Many adults have come to enjoy the benefits that alcohol can give. Alcohol's ability to decrease the nervous system's level of alertness may help people to relax. And by interfering with the brain's normal function of restraining impulses, it helps some people to be more open in talking with others. These effects have helped make alcohol a popular feature, and sometimes the main feature, of many parties.

Alcohol has come to be accepted as a natural part of entertainment. The average American now drinks more alcohol than milk. People go to a bar to unwind from a stressful week. They drink a few beers while cheering on their favorite sports team at the ball park. Weddings and reunions often feature an open bar that livens up the mood of the guests. Couples who do not normally drink alcohol with their meals order wine as part of a splurge at a fancy restaurant.

Symbol of rebellion

Widespread acceptance of alcohol among adults sends the message to teens that drinking is a positive activity. Some of them find themselves attracted to the same features that attract adults. Alcohol makes them feel more relaxed and confident, less anxious and inhibited. But beyond its role as a companion for entertainment and parties, alcohol has a hold on society as one of its main symbols of rebellion. Virtually everyone concedes the harmful effects of alcohol. Millions of people become addicted to it and spend their lives in a futile attempt to escape its clutches. The Centers for Disease Control estimate that nearly 100,000 Americans die each year from the effects of alcohol. The substance has destroyed families, careers, lives, and even societies.

Yet even in the face of this, alcohol has traditionally been regarded in many circles as harmless, or even as a

joke. Bragging about how much a person is going to drink or did drink is common. Heavy drinkers are often viewed as comical, adventurous, fun-loving spirits. At worst, society views drinking as a normal human weakness. Those who oppose drinking are often stereotyped as humorless busybodies who like to run other people's lives. Alcohol has come to stand as a symbol of independence against such spoilsports.

This makes alcohol especially attractive to youth, who often have the urge to rebel against the restrictions that adults place on them. Even teens who are well aware of the dangers of alcohol may drink as a way of expressing their independence. Adults encourage this by shrugging off even binge drinking among teens as just "kids being kids."

Some entertainers build up a teen audience by appealing directly to this rebellious instinct. This can result in

Drinking has become a way for many people to relax, unwind, and be less inhibited around their friends and others.

the promotion of drinking as the "cool" thing to do. Robert DuRant of the Bowman Gray School of Medicine at Wake Forest University found that at least 20 percent of the music videos shown on television included some form of alcohol use. In three out of four of these cases, drinking was presented as positive. According to DuRant, nearly 10 percent showed the use of alcohol by someone who appeared to be well under the legal drinking age. Such videos reinforce the view that drinking alcohol is the "in" thing to do.

Advertising: persuading people to drink

Alcoholic beverages are not only a common part of society, but they are part of a large industry that employs 2 million people in the United States. Americans spend more than $20 billion directly on alcoholic beverages and probably another $80 million on businesses that depend on alcohol. With so much money at stake, those in the alcohol industry have a huge interest in attracting and keeping customers. Critics note that the alcoholic beverage industry is in the awkward position of depending on a social problem to stay in business. While beer, wine, and liquor companies publicly promote responsible drinking, they would suffer crippling losses of income if all problem drinkers started drinking moderately.

Alcoholic beverage companies actively promote their products in the mass media. Beer advertisements make up nearly 5 percent of all commercials on television and more than 7 percent of all radio advertisements. The people in these commercials using alcohol are usually attractive, popular, athletic people—the kind of people most teens would like to be. Beer companies have a long tradition of associating their product with the most popular sporting events, which helps promote beer drinking as something that "real men" do.

Industry executives argue that their ads are designed to attract drinkers of other brands to their brand and to keep their customers loyal to their product. Yet future sales depend on attracting new customers. As one management consultant notes, "Everything the companies do is now geared much more to their younger audience."[17] This audience includes teens who are not legally permitted to drink.

Writing for *Business Week*, David Leonhardt concluded that liquor companies have directly targeted teens. "Liquor companies have a presence in virtually every publication with a sizable teen audience,"[18] he notes. As an example, he cites the music magazine *SPIN*. About 30 percent of *SPIN*'s readers are under eighteen years of age; nearly half are under the legal drinking age of twenty-one. Yet the magazine is filled from cover to cover with liquor ads.

Analysts point to cartoonish labels and mascots and game-filled websites sponsored by alcoholic beverage companies as selling techniques designed to appeal more to teens than to adults. The same is true of new products such as alcopops, which taste like lemonade but contain the same alcohol content as beer.

The fact that companies are willing to spend over $1 billion a year on advertisements is strong evidence that advertising is effective in persuading people to use the product. Ad experts note that in the face of several decades of heavy advertising by liquor, beer, and soft drink companies, young people overwhelmingly prefer to spend money on these products rather than drink water, which is not only healthier but free of charge.

Why teens drink and drive

Although teens may drink for many reasons, no one drinks because they want to drive drunk. Drunk driving happens because people who drink find themselves in the position of having to transport themselves in a vehicle. Teen drunk driving occurs in large numbers not only because many teens drink but because teens are so dependent on automobiles for transportation.

People in the United States own almost a third of all automobiles in the world. There is one automobile for every 1.4 persons in the country, compared with the worldwide average of 1 per every 10 persons. Owning an automobile has virtually become a necessity for participating fully in

American society. The spreading of the population from cities into the suburbs has greatly contributed to the need for automobiles. In a densely packed urban area, mass transit such as buses and subways provides the most efficient transportation. Stores can be maintained within walking distance of large numbers of customers. But the widely spread houses of the suburbs make mass transit less workable. Suburbs have replaced corner stores with malls, built on cheap land at the edges of the communities, that can be reached only by automobile.

Operation of an automobile has become an important symbol of status and self-esteem for American teens. A driver's license is one of the earliest privileges of adulthood granted to teens. Because they are no longer dependent on adults to take them where they need or want to go, teens with driver's licenses enjoy considerably more freedom than teens who do not drive.

Beer companies such as Anheuser-Busch have directly targeted teens and young adults through the use of mascots like Budweiser's talking frogs.

Deadly gamble

But along with the freedom that owning a driver's license provides comes a serious responsibility that carries the potential for tragedy. Safe operation of a vehicle requires not only training but maturity, judgment, and experience. By developing a lifestyle in which teens are heavily dependent on the private automobile, Americans have shown that they are willing to gamble that beginning drivers have enough judgment and maturity to make up for their lack of experience. For thousands of young drivers, it is a gamble that they lose—at the cost of their lives and the lives of their victims. Motor vehicle accidents are the number one killer of teens in the United States. They cause roughly one-third of all deaths of young people ages fifteen to twenty. Statistics show that teen drivers are at far greater risk behind the wheel than are older, more experienced drivers. More nineteen-year-olds are killed in traffic accidents than any other age group, with eighteen-year-olds right behind. According to the NHTSA, drivers ages fifteen to twenty made up only 7.1 percent of the driving population in 1996, yet they accounted for 14.9 percent of all driver fatalities.

As a society in which teens are almost completely dependent on the automobile for transportation, the United States has put inexperienced drivers at grave risk. The addition of alcohol, whose effects make driving many times more difficult, greatly multiplies the risk factor. Yet, by accepting and even encouraging the use of alcohol, Americans have made it easy for alcohol to enter the picture.

Bad examples

One reason why teens drink and drive is that adults have set a poor example. Approximately 1.5 million Americans will be arrested this year for driving while intoxicated, the vast majority of them adults. A 1990 study in Minnesota found that 8 percent of all licensed drivers had one or more drunk driving violations on their record.

Yet even this is only the tip of the iceberg. The number of people caught and charged with driving while intoxicated is only a small fraction of the number of people who drink and drive. In a poll of business executives under the age of fifty, 85 percent admitted they had driven while drunk. Safety experts estimate that close to 20 percent of the drivers in the United States drive while legally intoxicated at least once a year.

Perhaps the most dangerous impression that adults pass on to young drivers is that drinking beer and driving is not a problem. But, in fact, more than 60 percent of those convicted of driving while intoxicated report drinking only beer. Many of them express surprise that drinking beer could put them over the legal BAC limit.

Inexperience with drinking

By setting a relatively high BAC level at which driving is considered both legal and acceptable, states have created a situation in which young drivers unintentionally drive drunk. Teens have been taught that drinking and driving is safe as long as one knows one's limits. However, many adults have difficulty determining exactly how much they can drink and safely drive; the problem is greatly multiplied for teens who have had little or no experience with drinking.

Inexperienced drinkers may not notice the effect that alcohol is having on their nervous systems. In fact, drinking alcohol clouds the judgment they need to determine whether they are in any condition to drive. Worse yet, alcohol blocks some of the nerve impulses that govern restraint and caution. This means people who have been drinking are more inclined to take chances. They tend to feel confident and in complete control of the situation. The result is that many teens who drink badly overestimate their ability to operate a motor vehicle.

Inexperienced drivers

Statistics show that young drivers are actually more responsible than adults when it comes to drinking and driving. A smaller percentage of teens take to the road in an intoxicated condition. Unfortunately, those who do are more likely than adults to pay for their mistakes. According to James Jacobs, "While fewer young drivers drink, those who do are more dangerous drivers and are significantly overrepresented among traffic fatalities."[19] Young drivers have especially high accident rates at low BAC levels compared with adults.

Technically, teens have better driving skills than most other age groups. Their eyesight and reactions are superior to those of older drivers. They have more accidents simply because they lack driving experience. This inexperience means that they are more likely to get themselves into situations that require quick reactions, one of the responses that is dulled even by low BACs. Teens' inexperience in judging the speed and distance of an approaching car gives them less of a margin for error. That small margin may disappear altogether when their judgment is impaired by alcohol.

Disregard for consequences

Both teens and adults often drive drunk because of their lack of concern over consequences. Tragic collisions are

The idea that beer does not affect driving is a dangerous one.

viewed as freak accidents that happen to other people. In fact, the vast majority of trips taken by drunk drivers do not end in tragedy. Most of the time, nothing happens at all. Once a person has driven while intoxicated with no harm, it is easier to do it a second time.

When the likelihood of disaster seems remote, it is easy for teens to give in to the peer pressure that comes with that age. Not only will many teens drive after drinking, but they will also get into vehicles with unsafe drivers. Only when tragedy strikes do they realize that the consequences are so enormous that they are not worth even a tiny risk.

Every year, thousands of teens find that out the hard way. Anne was one of these. During her senior year of high school, Anne broke up with her boyfriend. Trying to pull her out of her depression over the situation, Anne's friends took her to a local restaurant. There she happened to see her boyfriend's older brother, Fred, sitting at the bar.

Anne spoke to Fred, who said he was sure his brother would be interested in getting back together with her. He offered to take her to him that night so that they could make up. Recognizing that Fred had obviously had too much to drink, Anne hesitated to go with him. But fearful of missing her opportunity to regain her boyfriend, she took the chance.

Less than half a mile from the restaurant, Fred's black Corvette crossed the center line and slammed head-on into an approaching vehicle. Fred died instantly; Anne died a week later on her eighteenth birthday.

4

The Law and Drunk Driving

MORE PEOPLE IN the United States are arrested for driving under the influence (DUI) than for any other reason. In 1996 this offense accounted for one out of every ten arrests in the country, a total of nearly 1.5 million citations. Taken together with the staggering death toll from drunk drivers, this statistic supports the statement by well-known criminal defense lawyer Alan Dershowitz: "The most serious crime in America is not drug use, or rape or armed robbery. It is drunken driving."[20]

On the other hand, some legal experts argue that drunk driving, by itself, should not be considered a crime at all. They maintain that drunk driving is a traffic offense, which is different from a crime. Unlike for criminal offenses, traffic offenders are not arrested and charged with a crime. Traffic violations can be cleared up by paying a fine, without formal hearings, or a trial. A person who fails to notice a stop sign, drives ten miles over the speed limit, or parks too long at a regulated parking space can hardly be branded a criminal.

Careless driving or criminal offense?

Critics of drunk driving laws note that traffic laws are concerned only with actual violations such as speeding, failure to stop, reckless driving, and so on. They maintain that what *causes* a person to speed, fail to stop, or drive recklessly should make no difference. Drunk driving appears to

Some people believe that driving while intoxicated is a more serious crime than drug use, rape, or armed robbery.

be a glaring exception to that rule. Drunk drivers may be arrested even if they are observing all the traffic rules.

Law-enforcement authorities argue that drunk drivers *should* be arrested even if they are driving legally because they pose a threat to those around them. Critics counter that sleepy or inattentive drivers pose a risk as well, but no one would consider arresting someone simply for being tired. In no case other than drunk driving does the traffic law allow a person to be arrested for something that *might* happen. The critics say that it would make more sense to eliminate the charge of drunk driving altogether and simply prosecute drunk drivers for the violations and crimes they commit while driving drunk.

Those who support singling out drunk driving as a separate offense argue that everyone has a duty to drive as safely as they possibly can. By the very act of drinking, a person knowingly takes action that reduces his or her ability to drive safely. Furthermore, drunk drivers pose such an increased risk for accidents that they endanger the public safety. Arresting them only when they actually commit an offense would be like allowing people to fire guns at random along a street and arresting them only if they actually hit somebody.

Blood alcohol content as proof

Until the development of chemical tests in the late 1940s, a drunk driving charge was similar to a reckless driving charge. Both were judgment calls based on certain behaviors. Drunk driving, however, was more difficult to prove because it involved not just actions but the actual physical condition of the accused.

Once chemical tests that determined a person's blood alcohol content were made available to law-enforcement officials, the matter of drunkenness was easy to prove. It was then up to the governments to decide what level of BAC diminished a person's ability to drive so severely that he or she should not be allowed behind the wheel.

Until the 1970s, most states used .15 as the BAC limit at which a person was considered intoxicated. This lenient standard meant that a person could down a twelve pack of beer or seven strong drinks in a couple of hours and still legally drive. As public awareness of drunk driving rose, most states dropped their standard to .10. In recent years, several states have joined Canada in lowering the threshold even lower to .08. Scandinavian countries have set .05 as the legal limit for driving.

Since teenagers cannot legally drink in the United States, the legal BAC limits do not apply to them in the same way. In 1995, the U.S. Congress passed legislation that required all states to pass "zero tolerance" laws for young drivers. Within two years, about forty-four states had done so. These laws declare that a teen with a BAC of .02, about the smallest amount of alcohol that can be reliably measured by normal police techniques, is in violation of the law.

Getting caught

For most of the century, the only way for police to stop and arrest drunk drivers was to catch them in a traffic violation or in the act of driving dangerously. People who drink and drive at moderate BAC levels, and even many at high levels, do not always show obvious signs of drunkenness, such as weaving across lanes. That meant that the vast majority of those who drank and drove went undetected. Experts estimate that the odds of being arrested for driving under the influence are less than 1 in 1,000 trips and less than 1 in 5,000 miles of driving.

In an effort to crack down on drunk drivers, in the 1980s police started randomly stopping cars on the road and testing drivers for BAC. That effort stopped when the courts ruled that such actions violated the Fourth Amendment to the U.S. Constitution, which protects citizens from unreasonable search. However, the courts did allow roadblocks, as long as drivers were warned that a checkpoint was ahead and police stopped all cars instead of singling out certain drivers for special treatment.

In recent years, many states have used roadblocks to catch drunk drivers. As part of a "Booze It and Lose It" campaign, North Carolina set up thousands of roadblocks a year in the mid-1990s. Jamirius Cureton had the misfortune of driving his Honda Civic in the Monroe, North Carolina, area after drinking beer in 1997. Despite signs warning of the roadblock ahead, he continued driving along the moderately traveled road until he was stopped by one of twenty-eight officers on hand. For most motorists, the delay lasted only a minute or two, while BAC tests were processed in a $200,000 mobile laboratory aboard a

A police officer watches as a driver stopped at a roadblock takes a coordination test.

converted school bus. Other than seat belt violations, the officers found very few traffic violations that evening. Only one driver tested over the state's BAC limit of .08. That offender was immediately taken to jail.

Cureton tested under the .08 standard. But as an eighteen-year-old, he was not legally allowed to drink at all and so he paid the penalty of a suspended license for one year.

The breathalyzer

The test that police asked Cureton to take was a breathalyzer test, which is standard procedure whether a driver is pulled over because of suspicious driving or as part of a roadblock. Because traffic regulations differ from criminal law, the person stopped does not have the normal rights granted to those accused of a crime. All states have passed what are commonly called "implied consent" laws. According to such laws, anyone who applies for a driver's license agrees to abide by the traffic laws in that state, including the requirement to provide a breath sample for alcohol testing. The penalty for not providing such a sample is generally automatic loss of license.

Breathalyzer analysis is based on the scientific finding that there is a direct ratio between the amount of alcohol in the blood and the amount in the air in the lungs. The BAC is figured by multiplying the amount of alcohol in the breath by 2,100. To test a driver's BAC, the driver blows into the mouthpiece of a device until he has emptied his lungs in one breath. The breathalyzer device traps only the last portion of the air sample, which is the air that comes directly from the lungs.

This sample is forced through a small tube that contains a solution of sulfuric acid and potassium dichromate. As the air bubbles through the yellow liquid, the sulfuric acid extracts the alcohol. The potassium dichromate then changes the alcohol to acetic acid. This change causes the yellow liquid to change color. The amount of color change is measured by photoelectric cells, and a mathematical formula converts that figure to the BAC. The breathalyzer provides a fairly accurate quick estimate of BAC. When

A nurse monitors the results of a breathalyzer test.

necessary, police obtain a sample of blood, which can provide a more precise analysis.

Legal consequences

A teen arrested for driving after drinking may face a number of charges, depending on the circumstances and the damage that results. The most common charges are driving while intoxicated (DWI) and underage drinking. The punishment for first-time offenders in the more routine cases usually involves a fine and suspension of license, and possibly probation.

If property damage occurs as a result of intoxication, the offender will have to pay for the damages. Repeat offenders and those who are more seriously drunk are likely to face stiffer penalties—higher fines, jail terms, longer probation, and loss of license. Scandinavian countries have a separate charge of "aggravated driving while intoxicated" for those whose BAC is above .15. This charge carries a prison sentence, whereas normal DWI involves only a fine.

Loss of life as a result of the actions of a drunk driver can bring criminal charges as well, most commonly manslaughter. Manslaughter is the act of causing another person's death without the intent to do so. Conviction of manslaughter brings a jail term. Judges may also require offenders to perform a given number of hours of community service. This often takes the form of public appearances to serve as an example and a warning to other teens.

Judges may also impose special penalties designed to force offenders to take responsibility for the suffering they cause. Brandon Blenden, whose drunken driving killed four-year-old Whitney Lee, received a sentence of twenty years in prison. In addition, the court required him to write a $1 check to her parents every week for the next ten years as restitution. The money was not important, and in fact the Lees never cash the checks. But to an otherwise law-abiding person, the regular checks serve as a constant reminder of the Lees' unending loss.

Getting tough

In the past two decades, most of the emphasis in the fight against drunk driving has been on tougher laws and stricter penalties. Mothers Against Drunk Driving, for example, has focused much of its energy on longer and more frequent jail sentences and stiffer fines even for first-time offenders. At the peak of its influence in the late 1980s, MADD had more than 370 national chapters, a membership of nearly 20,000, and cash contributions of over $40 million per year.

In response to the lobbying efforts of MADD, RID, the National Highway Traffic Safety Administration, and other groups, most states in the past two decades have increased the probability and length of jail time for drunk drivers. Increased penalties for drunk drivers have great appeal to the public, which has been outraged by reports of drunk drivers with several prior convictions let loose on the streets with only a mild slap on the wrist. These punishments provide some sense of justice, however inadequate, for families whose loved ones have been victims of drunk drivers.

Such policies also appear to have the effect of getting the most dangerous drivers off the road and keeping them off.

Debate continues, however, as to how far the law should go in punishing those who make the mistake of drinking and driving. Several states have raised the charges that can be brought against a drunk driver to the level of murder. This has raised the question, Should drunk drivers who cause deaths be prosecuted in the same manner as criminals who intentionally murder their victims?

Murder charges

For many decades, states treated cases of death caused by drunk drivers differently from other manslaughter cases. The penalties were more lenient. But as incidents of irresponsible drinking produced outrage over local deaths, more than a dozen states passed laws allowing those who killed while driving drunk to be convicted of murder—the intentional killing of another. Although the death was obviously not planned, legislatures declared that the extreme recklessness of driving a car while drunk indicated such a disregard for human life that a murder charge was justified. In 1976, a man in Montgomery, Alabama, who caused a death by drunk driving was convicted of first-degree murder by a jury and sentenced to life in prison. The Alabama Supreme Court, however, struck down the verdict. By the 1980s, discouraged by such opinions, district attorneys stopped prosecuting drunk drivers as murderers in all states except Alabama and Tennessee.

However, as public awareness of drunk driving grew during the 1980s, states began to get bolder in a renewed effort to prosecute drunk driving deaths as murder.

More than a horrible accident

One of the most publicized drunk driving cases centered on the actions of Thomas Jones, who had been taking a prescription drug to relieve the pain he suffered ever since losing part of his leg in a lawn mower accident. As Jones was well aware, this drug had a severe effect on his nervous system when combined with alcohol. Yet on the

evening of September 4, 1996, he drank beer after taking his medication and then stepped into his Nissan Altima.

Jones's head began swimming so badly that he could not keep the car in its lane. He bumped another car twice. He veered to the right and struck the curb so hard he nearly flipped over. Instead of recognizing his inability to operate the vehicle, he continued on. At about 10:30 P.M., he turned onto a two-lane road and again wandered over the center divider, traveling at least ten miles an hour over the thirty-five-mile-per-hour speed limit.

Fionna Penney was driving in the opposite direction on her way to a party. With her were five friends, all students at Wake Forest University. When she saw Jones speeding directly toward her, she cranked the wheel hard to the left to turn onto a side street. Just at that moment, though, Jones steered back into his lane. Before Penney could complete the turn, Jones rammed broadside into her Mazda. Penney and three others were injured in the crash. Julie Hanson and Maia Witzl did not survive.

Many states now consider deadly accidents involving alcohol to be acts of murder.

A blood test performed shortly after the accident found Jones's BAC to be only .051, under North Carolina's .08 limit. Yet the effects of alcohol combined with the painkiller were obvious. Furthermore, this was not the first time Jones had endangered lives with his drinking. He had been convicted of drunk driving twice before and had recently been charged a third time.

Prosecutors charged Jones with first-degree murder, even though no one accused him of intentionally killing the students. Under the North Carolina law, if a driver willfully took actions that put other lives at extreme risk, prosecutors did not have to show actual intent. North Carolina law also permitted the death penalty when murder was committed in the course of committing another felony. Noting that repeat drunk driving was a felony, prosecutors sought the death penalty. "Everybody needs to wake up and realize that these things don't just happen by accident,"[21] argued the prosecutors. It was the first time in American history that a jury was asked to sentence a person to death for drunk driving.

The jury had no trouble convicting Jones of the murders, but the death sentence was a different matter. As Andrew Leipold, a law professor at Duke University, explained, "We give the death penalty to people we're afraid of, to people that are different from us. And drunk drivers aren't, because they're our neighbors, or they're us."[22] Even the parents of the victims did not want Jones to be executed. In the end, the jury did not demand that Jones pay for his mistake with his life. But they did not let him off the hook. Jones received a sentence of two life terms without the possibility of parole.

Confiscating vehicles

The Jones case is an example of the government's recent trend to curb drunk driving by getting tough with drunk drivers. A similar example took place in New York City in 1999. Taking advantage of a law designed to strike at hardcore drug dealers, Mayor Rudolph Giuliani announced that the city would set up roadblocks and confiscate the cars of those accused of drunk driving, even first-time offenders. "It isn't punishment," Giuliani explained. "It's remedial."[23]

New York attorneys claimed the city was within its rights because it can confiscate property used in the course of committing a crime, and cars are obviously used in the course of drunk driving. They noted that one of their first roadblocks caught Francisco Almonte, a man with five DWI convictions and a BAC of .19. Impounding his car seemed the only way to get a hazard such as Almonte off the road.

But the measure has drawn many critics. They note that even if a driver is found not guilty in court, the drivers still have to go through civil court proceedings to win back their cars. Norman Seigal of the New York Civil Liberties Union declared the policy "excessive and unAmerican." Former Queens district attorney Dino Lombardi agreed, calling the penalty "grossly out of proportion to the crime."[24]

As an example of the unfairness, critics pointed to another of the first victims of the policy, a Russian immigrant

Mayor Rudolph Giuliani of New York has introduced a get-tough policy against drunk driving.

on his way home from the birthday party of a friend's one-year-old. His BAC was barely above the legal limit, at .11, and the man had never been arrested for drunk driving. Even though he desperately needed his car to get to work the city took it.

Tougher BAC standards

Several states have attempted to expand the laws against drinking and driving to include lowering the allowable BAC to .08, and most other states are under pressure from public interest groups to follow suit. The reasoning behind the move is that drivers with a blood alcohol content of between .08 and .10 are dangerous to the public, yet police can do nothing about them.

Such attempts face strong opposition from the liquor, restaurant, and bar industries, however, who warn that the lower BAC limit would make criminals of moderate drinkers. They also worry that those who want to lower the BAC levels are gradually bringing about their own form of Prohibition. Manufacturers of alcoholic beverages and their allies doubt that public interest groups will be satisfied with reducing the minimum BAC to .08. They fear that these people will keep pushing to lower the acceptable BAC level for driving to zero. They argue that this is not only unnecessary but would infringe on people's freedom and cause terrible economic loss to thousands of people.

Even some groups concerned with reducing drunk driving question whether lowering the allowable BAC is a good thing. They fear that such campaigns may actually hurt their efforts by creating angry opposition from the majority of Americans who drink moderately.

Does getting tough work?

The strategy of passing tougher penalties has two goals: to raise the cost of drinking and driving so high that few people will risk the consequence and to provide victims with a sense of justice. However, while tougher laws may provide some small comfort to families of drunk driving victims, according to Laurence Ross, "Little in the way of

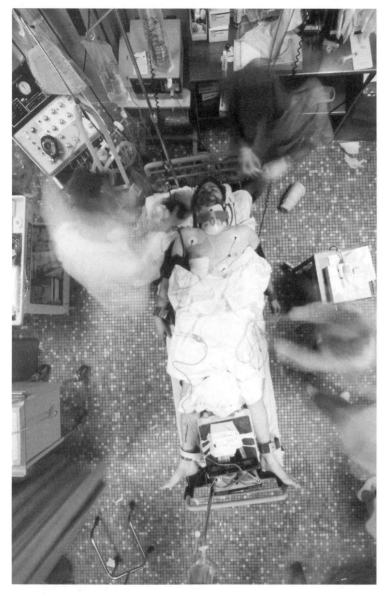

Doctors try to revive a victim of a drunk driver. Extensive fines or jail terms are not likely to stop people who are determined to risk lives by drinking and driving.

reduced drunk driving has been found in most studies of enacted jailing policies." [25]

One of the main reasons for this is a simple matter of logic. How can society raise the stakes for driving drunk any higher than they already are? Individuals who are determined to risk their life, the lives of friends and family who drive with them, and the lives of others on the road by drinking and driving are not likely to be scared off by the risk of increased jail time or a larger fine.

Furthermore, people who make the decision to drive drunk do not have control of the judgment and inhibition functions of their brain when they make that decision. In many cases, they are not capable of taking into account the increased consequences of deciding to drive while intoxicated. Without incentives or penalties to control drinking in the first place, getting tough will not have much effect in persuading people not to drive when drunk.

Another flaw of increased penalties is that they assume drunk driving problems are caused by a small minority of criminally irresponsible individuals. But although the typical drunk driver is thought of as a person who continues to drive while seriously impaired despite several arrests, most of those arrested for driving while intoxicated are otherwise respectable individuals with no prior arrests. Critics of drunk driving crackdowns ask what is to be gained from putting otherwise productive and law-abiding citizens behind bars for long periods of time.

Finally, increasing the penalties for drunk driving does not deal with the reasons why people drink and drive in the first place. As horrible as the effects of drunk driving may be, there is a limited amount of money that society is willing to spend on the problem. Critics of "get tough" laws argue that this limited money would be better spent on preventing people from driving drunk than on punishing them after the damage has been done.

5

Preventing Drunk Driving Tragedies

EXPERTS ON CRIMINAL behavior point out that consequences tend to affect people's behavior only if they are swift and certain. As it stands, only a tiny percentage of drunk drivers are unlucky enough to be stopped and arrested. People have good reason to believe that, no matter how high the penalties for drunk driving, they are not likely to be caught and therefore do not need to change their behavior. For this reason, some propose that law-enforcement efforts should concentrate on stopping and arresting more of those who drive drunk rather than increasing the penalties.

Discouraging drinking and driving through roadblocks

One method of law enforcement that is now being used more frequently to discourage people from drinking and driving is the roadblock. North Carolina's impressive road-block campaign is the reason why, according to reporter Matthew Wald: "North Carolina is the state the Federal safety experts cite as a national model in the campaign against drunk drivers."[26] When the state started the road-block campaign, law-enforcement officials found that about 2 percent of those stopped were legally intoxicated. Within a year, that number had dropped to less than 1 percent. State officials believe they have cut their state's drunk driving rate to the lowest in the nation. Insurance companies agree and have dropped the state's insurance premiums significantly.

Australia has obtained similar results with an even more ambitious program. One of its provinces hired two hundred extra police to stop and test hundreds of thousands of drivers each year. The result was a decline of 20 percent in the number of drunk drivers, and that decline has held steady. Monroe, North Carolina, police chief Bobby Haulk believes that the reason for the success of roadblocks is that they catch many drunk drivers who otherwise would be endangering lives. "You take enough of them off the road, you're going to save somebody,"[27] said Haulk.

But even massive roadblock efforts actually remove only a small fraction of the drunk drivers from the road. Safety experts argue that in both North Carolina and Australia, publicity was the key factor to reducing drunk driving. The roadblocks' main value lies in alerting the public that the chances of being arrested for driving while intoxi-

Signs posted on taxicabs are part of Australia's ambitious efforts to curb drunk driving.

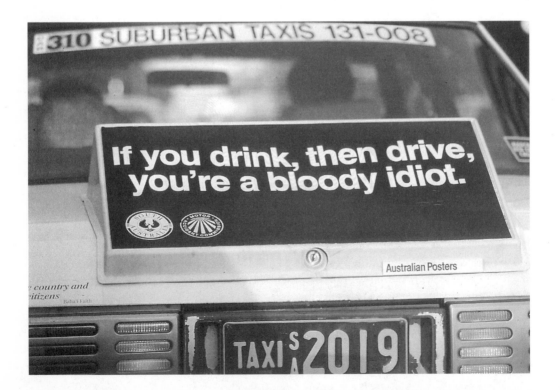

cated have increased dramatically, thus causing them to change their behavior.

The two major objections to roadblocks are the cost and the threat to freedom. An effective roadblock campaign requires the services of many police officers. James Hall, chairperson of the National Transportation Safety Board, notes that they require "putting the political will and the dollars behind enforcement."[28] The public may not be willing to pay the millions of dollars in taxes needed to pay these officers. When a roadblock patrolled by twenty-eight officers makes only two arrests in an entire evening, as reported by *New York Times* reporter Matthew Wald, people question whether the effort is worth the cost. Critics of roadblocks also express concern over the state's ability to stop and question law-abiding citizens whenever it chooses. Such practices put the nation closer to a police state in which the government keeps tight control over the activities of all citizens.

License suspension

Studies have shown that the most effective way to prevent drunk drivers from repeating their offense is to suspend their licenses. This keeps many of the most dangerous drivers off the road for a period of time. Furthermore, the inconvenience of not being able to drive in American society is a constant reminder of the folly of drunk driving, as opposed to paying a fine and then forgetting about it.

The problem with this has been that the risk of being caught driving with a suspended license is small. Many suspended drivers would rather run the risk than be without a car. In 1980, the state of California discovered that illegal drivers were involved in almost 40 percent of all fatal accidents. Some California cities responded by taking the cars of those driving without a license and keeping them for up to thirty days. Such a program helped San Francisco reduce fatal crashes involving drunk drivers by nearly 80 percent in 1995. Other states have stepped up enforcement by replacing the license plates on the vehicles of those

whose licenses have been suspended with plates that can be easily identified by police.

Reducing drinking

The high cost of law enforcement and the difficulty in stopping and arresting drunk drivers before they do damage prompt some to look at the original source of the drunk driving problem: alcohol. There is no question that for the luxury of drinking alcoholic beverages society pays a steep price that goes far beyond drunk driving. The Centers for Disease Control and Prevention estimate that every year in the United States nearly 100,000 people die from alcohol-related causes. While there is virtually no national support to ban alcoholic beverages, efforts have been made to reduce the amount of alcohol consumed.

One proposal is to raise taxes on alcohol. A severe price hike for alcoholic beverages would discourage people from buying them as frequently. Furthermore, it would force the price of the product to more closely cover the enormous costs of alcohol abuse to society. Those opposed to a high tax argue that the costs to society are almost completely the result of those who misuse alcohol and that responsible drinkers should not be forced to pay them.

Preventing teen drinking

According to Jim Mosher of the Marin Institute, an antidrug organization, "The earlier you begin drinking, the more likely you are to have alcohol problems and drunk driving problems."[29] Research shows that a person who begins drinking before the age of fifteen is four times as likely to develop an addiction to alcohol as someone who begins drinking at twenty-one.

This suggests that one of the most effective ways to reduce drunk driving is to reduce the amount of drinking among young people. History has shown this to be correct. Raising the age at which young people can legally drink has been a key factor in reducing teen drunk driving in recent years. The number of alcohol-related traffic fatalities involving teens has dropped significantly since the legal drinking age in all states was raised to twenty-one.

Enforcement of the minimum drinking age law, however, has been lax in many communities. One experiment in Washington, D.C., found that underage drinkers were able to purchase beer in 97 percent of their attempts. Those who sell alcoholic beverages, whether in liquor stores or bars, are often untrained or lack the motivation to enforce laws against selling or serving alcohol to teens. Many advocate tighter regulations and enforcement to crack down on alcohol sales to underage drinkers. This includes making those who sell to minors liable for the damage caused by those minors.

Those who have studied the problems of teen drinkers, though, have found that parents are often the most important safeguard against teen drinking. The children of parents who drink are far more likely to drink than those whose parents do not. A survey of eighth graders in urban areas in Southern California found that children who were at home unsupervised were twice as likely to drink alcohol as those in homes where an adult was present.

Another proposal to reduce teen drinking is to limit advertising for alcoholic beverages, especially advertisements that appeal to teens. Presently, there are no laws that specifically ban or regulate ads for alcoholic beverages. The trend, in fact, is in the opposite direction. For the past forty years, the liquor industry has voluntarily stayed away from advertising on television. However, it has recently lifted that self-imposed ban, citing the disadvantage this policy has put it in compared with beer companies that regularly advertise on TV.

Reduce driving

Another way of getting at the problem of drunk driving is to reduce the need for people to drive. Laurence Ross insists, "As a society, we will have to depend somewhat less on the private automobile and indulge somewhat less in our drug of choice, alcohol."[30] Greater use of mass transit such as buses and trains would eliminate the necessity of many people's having to drive after they have been drinking. The government could discourage the use of automobiles by imposing a high tax on gasoline. This would be especially effective in reducing the amount of miles people drive for recreation, which is associated with a large percentage of drinking and driving.

Americans, however, have been extremely reluctant to reduce their driving. Social institutions have made the independent operation of a motor vehicle crucial to getting around in society. And Americans show no inclination to leave their spread-out quarters of the suburbs for the more compact quarters of the inner city. In fact, many communities have cut funds for mass transit. Whereas in most of the world, and even in past American generations, people walk to many destinations, most Americans today drive even if they have to travel only a few blocks. This is especially true of teenagers, to whom driving an automobile is a source of pride and status.

Eliminating driver's education

School driver's education programs have been in operation for decades in many states. Their purpose is to provide safety instruction for young people so that they will become better, safer drivers. But, according to the American Automobile Association, driver's education courses have been cut at nearly half the schools in the nation. Those that continue to offer such programs often hold them after school, and programs that used to be offered free now charge a substantial fee. At a time when many school districts face budget shortages and are looking for ways to cut costs, this trend is likely to continue.

One of the most surprising suggestions of experts is that the elimination of driver's education programs in school is a good thing. In the words of one writer, "No study has ever proven that drivers education . . . makes teenagers drive any safer."[31] In fact, the main result of providing readily available and inexpensive driver's training programs in the schools has been to encourage teens to get their licenses at an earlier age than many did in the past. Younger drivers means more accidents.

By making driver's education programs more expensive and less convenient, schools have postponed driving for many young people, with positive safety results. Connecticut, for example, has noted a decline in vehicle crashes in many of its school districts that have eliminated driver's education.

Reducing the opportunity to drink and drive

If people continue to drink and drive despite the risks and the consequences, an effective effort to reduce drunk driving must find ways to limit their opportunities to do so. Technology could help in this regard. There are now ignition locks available that prevent vehicles from starting until the driver has passed a breathalyzer test. As a condition of probation, some communities are beginning to install such locks on the cars of those convicted of driving while intoxicated.

Some of the most dangerous drinking and driving situations occur in places where drinking is the primary activity and yet the only way to reach the location is by driving several miles in a private vehicle. This is particularly true of bars and taverns located on the outskirts of town or in the countryside along a highway. Communities could establish zoning laws that require such businesses to locate closer to the population or in places served by mass transit. The argument against this is, again, that the irresponsible behavior of a few drinkers should not be allowed to limit the freedom of law-abiding citizens.

Raising the driving age

The most obvious way to keep young drivers away from situations that might cause them to exercise bad judgment such as drinking and driving is to raise the licensing age. New Jersey found that upping its licensing age to seventeen produced a significant drop in fatal motor vehicle accidents. Young people in Victoria, Australia, must be at least eighteen to get their license. Since starting this policy, Victoria has boasted the lowest rate of traffic fatalities per licensed driver of all Australian states.

More common than a simple raising of the licensing age is the graduated driver's license. Slightly more than half the states presently have some form of graduated licensing, and more states are considering joining them. The NHTSA backs the concept, which assumes that a license is a privilege to be earned over time rather than all at

Bars in remote locations that can only be reached by car add to the problem of drinking and driving.

once. According to Ann Drumm of the American Automobile Association's Southern California branch, "The whole idea is to postpone the exposure of new drivers to more dangerous driving conditions and give them time to gain real-life experience."[32] Typical of the program are Michigan's graduated licensing laws, which require students to pass several levels of experience before receiving a permanent, unrestricted license at seventeen.

Curfews and other restrictions

Curfews are one of the restrictions that graduated licensing programs often place on young people because night is the most dangerous time for young people to be on the road. Night driving requires more skill and experience even for sober drivers. Yet nighttime is when most drinking takes place. Less than 20 percent of the total number of miles that sixteen-year-olds drive are covered between the hours of 9 P.M. and 6 A.M., but over 40 percent of their fatalities occur during those same hours.

Because of this, some states have begun to restrict nighttime driving of very young drivers. In New York, for example, a sixteen-year-old's driver's license is valid only between the hours of 5 A.M. and 9 P.M. This restriction is removed at age seventeen only if the driver has not been cited for any traffic violations or been involved in any accidents.

Other graduated license policies require an adult to be present or prohibit young drivers from carrying passengers in the first few months of their driving. A proposal under consideration by the Wisconsin legislature calls for young drivers to log fifty hours of driving time accompanied by an adult before getting a permanent license. Among other benefits, this protects young drivers from the influence of friends who might urge them to drive after drinking. People under the age of eighteen are also banned from driving in New York City, where the busy traffic makes driving especially hazardous.

All the policies aimed at taking young drivers off the road spark protests from teens angered at having their freedom restricted. They are especially irked at the inconveniences such as being unable to go on a date or drive to work in their car. Some of them believe that the restrictions will cause more harm than good. "If you have to be in by 12, you might be speeding to get home on time,"[33] says Matt Schoh, a student in Elk Mound, Wisconsin.

Such protests are likely to fall on deaf ears. Restrictions on young drivers' licenses are likely to gain more acceptance than other attempts to crack down on drunk driving because sixteen-year-olds do not vote and so have no political power. But if adults expect teens to alter their lifestyle without making any effort to alter their own drinking and driving habits, they will only provide more incentive for teens to defy authority.

Changing attitudes

Attempts to regulate drinking and driving and the situations that lead to them face tough sledding unless the public overwhelmingly supports them. As Susan Herbel observes, "Until drunk driving gets to be a behavior that is just not socially acceptable, we're not going to stop it."[34]

North Carolina was able to install the most effective anti–drunk driving program in the nation because the state's citizens made it a high priority. Governor James Hunt, who was himself involved in a head-on collision with a drunk driver many years ago, featured the reduction of drunk driving as one of his major election issues.

Awareness of the problem of drinking and driving has received a boost in recent years from the entertainment and sports industries—both of which have considerable influence with teens. Popular television programs such as *Beverly Hills, 90210* and *The Cosby Show* have dealt with the issue of drunk driving. In 1999, the National Collegiate Athletic Association ran a blizzard of anti–drinking and driving TV ads during the national basketball championships. Such measures help to combat the idea that drinking and driving is acceptable behavior.

The Corrective Behavior Institute has taken more aggressive action in changing the attitude of teens who drink and drive. It has set up a program in San Diego in which juveniles convicted of driving under the influence must visit coroners' offices and emergency hospital units to get a close-up view of the horrifying consequences of driving drunk.

The key to awareness

Kevin Brockway had owned a driver's license for just five days when he drove off to a New Year's Eve party celebrating the arrival of 1998. Although his father, Tom, was

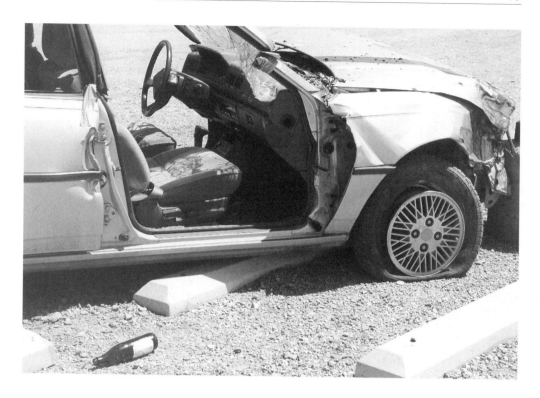

aware than Kevin had been sneaking alcohol at times during the year, he thought they had worked through that problem. "I thought I had a good handle of what Kevin was up to," said Tom. "But he became someone I didn't know during a two-hour period one night." [35]

That night, Kevin drank heavily at the party. He tried to drive himself and a passenger home. Just three blocks from his house in St. Paul, Minnesota, he lost control of his 1988 Celebrity, slammed into a tree, and was killed.

Through their grief and numbness, the Brockways tried to find a way to make something good come out of Kevin's death. His nineteen-year-old sister, Kristen, designed a key ring in the maroon and gold colors of Harding High School, where Kevin was a student. Inscribed on the ring were the words, "In memory of Kevin Brockway. Think of me—before you turn the key." [36]

The Brockways intended for the key rings to be a reminder only to Kevin's classmates at Harding. But after a local television station reported the effort, the Brockways

Accidents such as this one will continue to happen as long as drinking and driving is not considered to be socially unacceptable behavior.

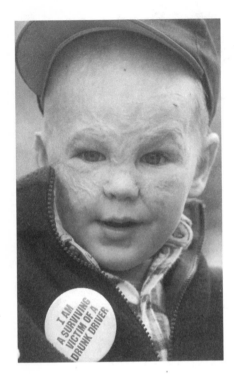

Three-year-old George Harmon helped in MADD's New Hampshire campaign against drunk driving. He was burned and his mother died when their car was hit by a drunk driver.

received requests for rings from around the state. Within the year, they sent out more than thirty-five thousand, each with a copy of the story of Kevin's tragedy, written by his father. Experts who warn against the dangers of drunk driving say that the message needs to be repeated time after time in order to be effective. The Brockways hope that, for those who own a key ring, it will serve as a vivid reminder of the consequences of drunk driving every time they start the car.

Responsible drinking

The alcoholic beverage industry has also made public relations efforts to curb drinking and driving, especially among teens. "Know your limits" and "know when to say when" are some of the more popular slogans they have promoted. Critics of the industry, however, wonder if these slogans do more harm than good. Both of them suggest that drinking alcohol is normal and even desirable. They leave the false impression that alcohol has no effect on normal activity, including driving, as long as drinkers do not go overboard.

Many bars sponsor designated driver programs, an idea that originated in Norway. The idea is for groups of drinkers to designate one of their members to avoid drinking for the evening. This person will be responsible for transporting other members home. Bars encourage this safety measure by providing free nonalcoholic beverages for the designated driver. Other bars look after the safety of their patrons by offering safe rides home.

Unfortunately, few drinkers in the United States take advantage of these types of programs. Participation in a safe ride program is too often avoided as a sign of weakness—a public admission that the drinker cannot handle his or her liquor or does not know when to say when. Many feel that designated driver programs impose a burden on the designated driver, who cannot join in the social activity of drinking with the rest of the group and must drive around to various houses at the end of the evening. There is also concern that these programs encourage heavy drinking among the nondrivers, which can lead to other dangerous consequences.

Friends and family

Another popular slogan of those working to reduce drunk driving is "friends don't let friends drive drunk." This approach has the advantage of bringing into play those who have not been drinking and whose consciences and judgment are bound to be functioning better than those of drinkers.

Students Against Destructive Decisions (SADD) tries to form a bond between parents and children that will prevent drinking and driving. The organization was founded in 1981 by Robert Anastas, a Massachusetts high school teacher. SADD has drawn up a contract to be signed by

This young woman has taken her friends' car keys to prevent them from driving drunk.

young people and their parents. The teen agrees to call the parents for a ride home if the teen or the person he or she depends on for a ride has been drinking. The parents agree to give them a ride, regardless of the time or place, and to postpone discussion of the incident to a later date.

Protecting those who do drink and drive

Given human nature and the modern lifestyle, there is no way to completely eliminate drunk driving. That being the case, some people argue that more effort should be made to protect those who do drink and drive from tragedy. The greatest dangers to drunk drivers are obstacles near the road. The removal of trees, telephone poles, and curbs from roadways reduces the chances of drunk drivers killing themselves or their passengers. Providing reflectors on curves and leveling out shoulders to remove steep embankments and ditches would accomplish the same thing.

Highway safety experts have been working for years to make roads and vehicles safer even for bad drivers. Their efforts, which have included antilock brake systems, seat belts, and air bags, have paid off. There has been a 90 percent reduction in the rate of highway deaths since the 1920s. The crash rate on the interstate highway system is half that of the highways it replaced despite the greater speed of traffic. Three decades ago, the U.S. death rate among motorists was 5.5 per 100 million miles driven. In recent years, the figure has held steady at 1.7, even though the roads are far more crowded than they were even a decade ago.

But experts warn that most of the safety steps that can be taken have already been put in place. Dr. Ricardo Martinez of the NHTSA puts the matter simply when he says, "What it comes down to now is driver behavior."[37]

Who is responsible?

In recent years, efforts have been made to curb drunk driving by spreading the responsibility. There have been proposals to require any business that serves alcohol to remain open an hour beyond the last serving of alcohol and to provide food to help customers sober up. Some have proposed making party hosts legally liable if one of their guests has an accident driving home drunk. Bills have been introduced in legislatures holding employers responsible for employees who drive home drunk from office parties.

Others believe that the responsibility for drinking and driving lies solely with the individual. Brian O'Neill, president of the Insurance Institute for Highway Safety, argues, "No one has any idea how to make drivers safe. It's not a question of skills, but of attitudes—what they choose to do behind the wheel."[38]

Choice is the key word. Individuals can choose not to drink or can refuse to put themselves in a position where they may have to drive if they drink. Regardless of the attitudes of society toward drinking and driving, there is one person who can stop someone from getting behind the wheel drunk: That is the driver.

Notes

Introduction

1. Quoted in Tim J. Sheehan, "McEwen Gets Six Months in Jail," *(Eau Claire) Leader-Telegram*, May 25, 1996, p. B-1.

2. Quoted in Sheehan, "McEwen Gets Six Months in Jail," p. B-2.

3. Quoted in Julian Emerson, "Students See How Alcohol, Cars Don't Mix," *(Eau Claire) Leader-Telegram*, April 20, 1996, p. B-1.

4. Quoted in Tim Sheehan, "DW Why? Son's Death Haunts, Motivates Father," *(Eau Claire) Leader-Telegram*, March 16, 1997, p. F-1.

Chapter 1: Unguided Missiles on the Road

5. Quoted in Matthew Wald, "Tough Action on Drunk Driving Pays Off," *New York Times*, November 26, 1997, p. A-1.

6. Quoted in Lesley Hazelton, "Fear Is Increasing on the Roads, but That May Not Be a Bad Thing," *New York Times*, October 16, 1997, p. G-2.

7. Quoted in Joey Kennedy, "Drunk Driving Makes a Comeback," *Redbook*, May 1997, p. 90.

8. Quoted in James B. Jacobs, *Drunk Driving: An American Dilemma*. Chicago: University of Chicago Press, 1989, p. xiv.

9. U.S. Department of Transportation, "Youth Fatal Crash and Alcohol Facts," 1994.

10. Quoted in Kennedy, "Drunk Driving Makes a Comeback," p. 89.

11. Quoted in Roberto Suro, "Dip in Youth Drug Use Hailed by Officials as Sign of Hope," *Washington Post*, August 7, 1997, p. A-4.

Chapter 2: How Drinking Affects Driving Ability

12. Vivian Begali, *Head Injury in Children and Adolescents*. Brandon, VT: Clinical Psychology, 1992, p. 42.
13. Jacobs, *Drunk Driving*, p. 78.
14. H. Laurence Ross, *Confronting Drunk Driving: Social Policy for Saving Lives*. New Haven, CT: Yale University Press, 1992, p. 3.
15. Quoted in Ross, *Confronting Drunk Driving*, p. 20.

Chapter 3: Who Drinks and Drives and Why

16. Quoted in Kennedy, "Drunk Driving Makes a Comeback," p. 90.
17. Quoted in David Leonhardt, "A Little Booze for the Kiddies," *Business Week*, September 23, 1996, p. 158.
18. David Leonhardt, "How Big Liquor Takes Aim at Teens," *Business Week*, May 19, 1997, p. 92.
19. Jacobs, *Drunk Driving*, p. 48.

Chapter 4: The Law and Drunk Driving

20. Quoted in Ross, *Confronting Drunk Driving*, p. 22.
21. Quoted in Kevin Sack, "Jury Holds a Drunk Driver's Life in the Balance," *New York Times*, May 6, 1997, p. B-9.
22. Quoted in Kevin Sack, "Jury Spares Drunk Driver from Death Penalty in Killing," *New York Times*, May 7, 1997, p. A-1.
23. Quoted in Gregory Beals, "Rudy Takes the Keys," *Newsweek*, March 8, 1999, p. 27.
24. Quoted in Beals, "Rudy Takes the Keys," p. 28.
25. Ross, *Confronting Drunk Driving*, p. 58.

Chapter 5: Preventing Drunk Driving Tragedies

26. Wald, "Tough Action on Drunk Driving Pays Off," p. A-1.
27. Quoted in Wald, "Tough Action on Drunk Driving Pays Off," p. A-1.
28. Quoted in Wald, "Tough Action on Drunk Driving Pays Off," p. A-24.

29. Quoted in Leonhardt, "A Little Booze for the Kiddies," p. 158.

30. Ross, *Confronting Drunk Driving*, p. 193.

31. Quoted in Jacques Steinberg, "Not the Driver's Ed Class Your Parents Remember," *New York Times*, October 16, 1997, p. G-2.

32. Quoted in Maria Casey, "Drunken Driving Pondered," *New York Times*, February 16, 1997, p. CN-4.

33. Quoted in Susan Barber, "License to Learn?" (*Eau Claire*) *Leader-Telegram*, March 11, 1999, p. C-1.

34. Quoted in Kennedy, "Drunk Driving Makes a Comeback," p. 90.

35. Quoted in Suzanne P. Campbell, "Think of Me," *Lutheran*, March 1999, p. 19.

36. Quoted in Campbell, "Think of Me," p. 19.

37. Quoted in Hazelton, "Fear Is Increasing," p. G-2.

38. Quoted in Steinberg, "Not the Driver's Ed Class Your Parents Remember," p. G-2.

Organizations
to Contact

American Automobile Association
Traffic Safety and Engineering Department
1000 AAA Dr.
Heathrow, FL 32746-5863
(407) 253-9100
www.aaa.com

The nation's largest service organization for drivers has a Foundation for Traffic Safety, which includes information on driver safety aimed at teen drivers.

Anheuser-Busch, Inc.
Consumer Awareness and Education
One Busch Pl.
St. Louis, MO 63118
(314) 577-2000

The nation's largest beer manufacturer has a public relations department that deals with drinking and societal issues. Among its services are speakers, programs, information, and links to other responsible drinking sources.

MADD (Mothers Against Drunk Driving)
511 East John Carpenter Freeway
Irving, TX 75062
(800) GET-MADD
www.madd.org

This is an intense, anti–drunk driving organization that advocates for victims of drunk drivers. It provides current news on the subject as well as programs and policy recommendations aimed at enforcing criminal sanctions against drunk drivers and protecting the rights of both victims and potential victims of drunk drivers.

Miller Brewing Co.
3939 West Highland Blvd.
P.O. Box 482
Milwaukee, WI 53201-0482
(414) 931-2000

Anheuser-Busch's major U.S. competitor in the beer market has a similar public relations program to promote responsible drinking and curtail drunk driving.

National Clearinghouse for Alcohol and Drug Information
P.O. Box 2345
Rockville, MD 20847-2345
(800) 729-6686
www.health.org

This is the world's largest resource for current information and materials on alcohol and alcohol abuse. Its information specialists can guide information seekers through the vast collection of free and low-cost materials to help them find what they are looking for.

National Commission Against Drunk Driving
1900 L St. NW, Suite 705
Washington, DC 20036
(202) 452-6004
www.ncadd.com

This is a nonprofit organization working to make drunk driving socially unacceptable. Resources include facts, tips on what individuals can do to combat drunk driving, and information on designated driver programs.

National Highway Traffic Safety Administration
Room 5118, NTS-13
400 Seventh St. SW
Washington, DC 20590
(202) 366-9550
www.nhtsa.gov

This government organization is the best source for current information, statistics, surveys, and trends in traffic safety, with extensive emphasis on the effects and frequency of drinking and driving.

RID (Remove Intoxicated Drivers)
P.O. Box 520
Schenectady, NY 12301
(518) 372-0034
www.crisny.org/not-for-profit/riduse

This is the oldest of the anti–drunk driving organizations. Because it spends so little on administration, it is less efficient at providing access to its resources. But it provides valuable materials, public awareness programs, and interactive media on the subject.

SADD (Students Against Destructive Decisions)
P.O. Box 800
Marlborough, MA 01752
(502) 481-3568
www.saddonline.com

This organization is specifically aimed at teens. It not only has reference materials and relevant information, but also provides a network for contacting other teens with the same concerns, help in starting new SADD chapters, and support in keeping them going.

Suggestions for Further Reading

Suzanne P. Campbell, "Think of Me," *Lutheran*, March 1999. Moving account of one family's tragic experience with teenage drinking and driving and how they strove to make something positive come of it.

Jean McBee Knox, *Drinking, Driving, and Drugs.* New York: Chelsea House, 1988. This book is geared to teenagers. It examines the effects of alcohol and other drugs on driving and provides some information on alcoholism. Also included is a series of sobering advertisements about drunk driving.

Judy Monroe, *Alcohol.* Springfield, NJ: Enslow, 1994. Easy-to-read book that details the history of alcohol use and its effects on the body and the mind, with plenty of statistics and personal anecdotes.

Richard Steins, *Alcohol Abuse: Is This Danger on the Rise?* Brookfield, CT: Twenty-First Century Books, 1995. For younger readers, an introduction to current trends in alcohol abuse, with full-color photos.

L. B. Taylor, *Driving High: The Hazards of Driving, Drinking, and Drugs.* New York: Franklin Watts, 1983. This book, written for young adult readers, is heavy on examples and anecdotes concerning teens who have driven drunk. Some of the information and statistics are dated.

Works Consulted

Books

Vivian Begali, *Head Injury in Children and Adolescents.* Brandon, VT: Clinical Psychology, 1992. This is a detailed treatment of the subject of brain injuries. It includes a great deal of information on how the brain works and how it responds to various outside influences.

Lawrence A. Greenfield, *Alcohol and Crime.* Washington, DC: Bureau of Justice Statistics, 1998.

James B. Jacobs, *Drunk Driving: An American Dilemma.* Chicago: University of Chicago Press, 1989. For more advanced readers, an in-depth look at the social influences and legal implications of drinking and driving.

H. Laurence Ross, *Confronting Drunk Driving: Social Policy for Saving Lives.* New Haven, CT: Yale University Press, 1992. Also for advanced readers, a thorough treatment of the myths and realities surrounding the issue of drinking and driving.

Periodicals

Susan Barber, "License to Learn?" (*Eau Claire*) *Leader-Telegram*, March 11, 1999.

Gregory Beals, "Rudy Takes the Keys," *Newsweek*, March 8, 1999.

Maria Casey, "Drunken Driving Pondered," *New York Times*, February 16, 1997.

Jen M. R. Doman, "For the Life of Your Daughter," *Life*, April 1997.

Julian Emerson, "Students See How Alcohol, Cars Don't Mix," (*Eau Claire*) *Leader-Telegram*, April 20, 1996.

Lesley Hazelton, "Fear Is Increasing on the Roads, but That May Not Be a Bad Thing," *New York Times*, October 16, 1997.

Joey Kennedy, "Drunk Driving Makes a Comeback," *Redbook*, May 1997.

David Leonhardt, "A Little Booze for the Kiddies," *Business Week*, September 23, 1996.

——, "How Big Liquor Takes Aim at Teens," *Business Week*, May 19, 1997.

Kevin Sack, "Jury Holds a Drunk Driver's Life in the Balance," *New York Times*, May 6, 1997.

——, "Jury Spares Drunk Driver from Death Penalty in Killing," *New York Times*, May 7, 1997.

Tim J. Sheehan, "McEwen Gets Six Months in Jail," (*Eau Claire*) *Leader-Telegram*, May 25, 1996.

Tim Sheehan, "DW Why? Son's Death Haunts, Motivates Father," (*Eau Claire*) *Leader-Telegram*, March 16, 1997.

Jacques Steinberg, "Not the Driver's Ed Class Your Parents Remember," *New York Times*, October 16, 1997.

Roberto Suro, "Dip in Youth Drug Use Hailed by Officials as Sign of Hope," *Washington Post*, August 7, 1997.

U.S. Department of Justice, "Drunk Driving," 1992.

U.S. Department of Transportation, "Youth Fatal Crash and Alcohol Facts," 1994.

Matthew Wald, "Tough Action on Drunk Driving Pays Off," *New York Times*, November 26, 1997.

Index

Picture Credits

About the Author

Nathan Aaseng has written more than one hundred books for young readers on a wide variety of subjects; more than two dozen of them have won awards. He lives in Eau Claire, Wisconsin, where he and his wife have piloted two children into the perilous world of teen driving, with two more waiting eagerly in the wings.